P9-DZZ-719

Understanding
How Students
Learn

WITHDRAWN

Leadership for Learning

Series Editors
Willis D. Hawley and E. Joseph Schneider

Joseph Murphy
Leadership for Literacy: Research-Based Practice, PreK–3

P. Karen Murphy and Patricia A. Alexander
Understanding How Students Learn: A Guide for Instructional Leaders

E. Joseph Schneider
The Principal's Guide to Managing Communication

Please call our toll-free number (800-818-7243)
or visit our Web site (www.corwinpress.com)
to order individual titles or the entire series.

P. Karen Murphy • Patricia A. Alexander

Understanding How Students
Learn

A Guide for
Instructional
Leaders

TOURO COLLEGE LIBRARY
Kings Hwy

CORWIN PRESS
A SAGE Publications Company
Thousand Oaks, California

KH

Copyright 2006 by Corwin Press.

All rights reserved. When forms and sample documents are included, their use is authorized only by educators, local school sites, and/or noncommercial or nonprofit entities who have purchased the book. Except for that usage, no part of this book may be reproduced or utilized in any form or by any means, electronic or mechanical, including photocopying, recording, or by any information storage and retrieval system, without permission in writing from the publisher.

For information:

Corwin Press
A Sage Publications Company
2455 Teller Road
Thousand Oaks, California 91320
www.corwinpress.com

Sage Publications Ltd.
1 Oliver's Yard
55 City Road
London EC1Y 1SP
United Kingdom

Sage Publications India Pvt. Ltd.
B-42, Panchsheel Enclave
Post Box 4109
New Delhi 110 017 India

Printed in the United States of America

Library of Congress Cataloging-in-Publication Data

Murphy, P. Karen.
Understanding how students learn: A guide for instructional leaders / P. Karen Murphy, Patricia A. Alexander.
    p. cm. — (Leadership for learning)
Includes bibliographical references and index.
ISBN 1-4129-0885-X (cloth) — ISBN 1-4129-0886-8 (pbk.)
    1. Learning. 2. Cognition in children. I. Alexander, Patricia A. II. Title. III. Series.
LB1060.M87 2006
370.15′23—dc22

                                        2005012565

This book is printed on acid-free paper.

05   06   07   08   09   10   9   8   7   6   5   4   3   2   1

Acquisitions Editor:	Rachel Livsey
Editorial Assistant:	Phyllis Cappello
Production Editor:	Melanie Birdsall
Typesetter:	C&M Digitals (P) Ltd.
Copyeditor:	Bill Bowers
Proofreader:	Mary Meagher
Indexer:	J. Naomi Linzer
Cover Designer:	Lisa Miller

7/6/06

Pricilla A. Murphy
J. W. Good III
. . . instructional leaders who touched our lives
and the lives of countless other teachers and students along the way.

In memory of
Bradford S. Woods
. . . our friend who always chose the road less taken.

Contents

List of Tables and Figures

Tables

Figures

Series Introduction

This book is one in a series being edited as part of the Leadership for Learning initiative of the American Association of School Administrators (AASA). Its primary purpose is to enhance the capacity of school leaders to improve the quality of teaching. By so doing they can ensure that all students learn at high levels.

If school leaders are to improve teaching, they must know how students learn. Furthermore, school leaders must understand what the implications of this knowledge are for effective teaching. Understandings of how students learn shape the behaviors of teachers, parents, and policy makers. Too often, however, these beliefs are incomplete, outdated, or involve misconceptions. This, of course, undermines school improvement.

The authors of this book are prominent educational psychologists whose careers have focused on understanding cognitive development. In this book they synthesize an extraordinary body of research to provide school leaders with knowledge they can use to know when students are learning, and when teaching reflects research on learning in the most productive ways. While the book focuses on student learning, the research examined here can also be used to design and implement effective professional development.

Often, books or articles meant to influence practice "translate" so-called technical terms used by researchers. Some terms used by experts are esoteric and unnecessarily obscure. But in many cases, the way experts describe phenomena deepens understanding. Without an awareness of the meaning of the language used by experts in the study of cognition, the ability of school leaders to enhance their own expertise is diminished. School leaders need to be experts with respect to how students learn. Thus, the authors of this book do not redefine the terms used by those who study how people learn. Instead, they provide tools for expert vocabulary building throughout the book.

This isn't a book that invites the school leader to "cherry-pick" an idea or two from the text for use the next day. It is a serious read that requires study and reflection.

In addition to outlining specific guidelines for research-based action, this book provides leaders with the understanding of how students learn that empowers them to work productively with teachers, parents, community leaders, and students. It helps leaders lead by facilitating the learning of others.

—*Willis D. Hawley*

Preface

What is blatantly clear in this new millennium is that school accountability for student learning outcomes is here to stay. Indeed, since the early 1980s, government reform initiatives have become the norm rather than the exception. Noticeably absent among all these potential reform initiatives, however, are the insights and understandings contained within the vast bodies of psychological research on teaching and learning. Indeed, in practice, the collective wisdom of psychology has exerted only limited influence in educational reform and everyday instructional practice. The lack of integration of psychological principles in educational reform initiatives has been due, in part, to psychology's failure to make its findings accessible and pertinent.

The purpose of this text is to do just that—make classic and current psychological understandings interpretable and relevant for instructional leaders and practicing teachers. Specifically, our intended audience is school administrators who have already assumed the mantle of instructional leader. We also believe that the ideas and recommendations captured in these pages can prove invaluable to those contemplating a career in school administration, or teachers concerned with student learning and academic development.

In this text, we take a learner-centered psychological approach in which we explore key psychological dimensions of learners in language that is accessible to instructional leaders and teachers. It is important to understand that "learner-centered" within this context does not correspond to any particular pedagogical orientation (e.g., discovery learning), as might be the case within the curriculum literature. Rather, learner-centered here signifies a focus on optimal learning for each and every student, whether preschooler or high-schooler or whether highly able or struggling learner.

Among the key dimensions we discuss in this volume are learner development; knowledge and understanding; learner motivation;

strategies and regulating learning; and shared learning. Each chapter begins with framing questions that came from *real* educational leaders trying to understand how psychology and education can come together to enhance learning for all students. The middle section of each chapter offers an overview of classic and current research from educational psychology and related areas like development, motivation, and policy. In our overview of relevant research, we specifically address each of the initial framing questions.

Moreover, each chapter ends with *principles for practice* in which we offer guiding principles that suggest ways instructional leaders can apply the particular dimension of learning to their own schools. In essence, we wanted to ensure that school administrators acting on these principles could operate with confidence that these ideas are much more than one's hopes, conjectures, or opinions, and are, in fact, evidence-based principles.

Acknowledgments

The thoughts, issues, advice, and support offered by friends, family, colleagues, and students were instrumental in writing this book. In particular we wish to thank:

Maeghan N. Edwards, The Pennsylvania State University
Jonna M. Kulikowich, The Pennsylvania State University
Rayne A. Sperling, The Pennsylvania State University
Anita Woolfolk Hoy, The Ohio State University
John F. Alexander, Ferguson Elementary School
Willis Hawley, University of Maryland
Rachel Livsey
Phyllis Cappello
CEBAS
Elaina and Yudi Hershowitz

The contributions of the following reviewers are gratefully acknowledged:

Catherine Payne
Principal
W. R. Farrington
   High School
Honolulu, HI

Sheri R. Parris
Doctoral Candidate
Reading Education
University of North Texas
Denton, TX

Diane Payne
Principal
Broughton High School
Raleigh, NC

Roxana Cardona
Assistant Principal
Public School 48
Bronx, NY

About the Authors

 **P. Karen Murphy** is an associate professor of Education in the Department of Educational and School Psychology and Special Education at The Pennsylvania State University. Her research focuses on learning and development, with a particular emphasis on the influence that beliefs, knowledge, and interest play in formal learning. Her current research projects pertain to the influence of students' knowledge and beliefs about learning from mathematics texts, the influence of technology in text-based comprehension, and the role of group discussions in high-level reading comprehension.

She has served as Program Chair and Chair of the Graduate Affairs Committee of Division 15 (Educational Psychology) of the American Psychological Association, and as a Section Chair and Chair-Elect of the Sylvia Scribner Award Committee of Division C (Learning and Instruction) of the American Educational Research Association. Since receiving her PhD from the University of Maryland in 1998, Dr. Murphy has published numerous articles in such prestigious journals as the *Educational Psychologist, Journal of Educational Psychology, Contemporary Educational Psychology,* and *Educational Researcher.* She has also coauthored multiple book chapters, including a recent chapter in the *Handbook of Educational Psychology.* In addition, Dr. Murphy is a regular presenter at national and international conferences, including the annual meetings of the American Psychological Association, American Educational Research Association, and National Reading Conference. Currently, Dr. Murphy serves on the editorial boards of *Contemporary Educational Psychology, Journal of Experimental Education,* and *Instructional Science,* and has served as a guest reviewer for *Journal of Educational Psychology, Educational Researcher, American Educational Research Journal, Educational Psychology Review,*

British Journal of Educational Psychology, Educational Psychologist, and *Theory Into Practice.*

Among her honors, Dr. Murphy has been the recipient of awards for her dissertation research from the American Psychological Association and the International Reading Association. In addition, has been honored with the Young Scholar of the Year Alumni Award by the College of Education at the University of Maryland, and has received the Probationary Faculty Research Award from both the School of Educational Policy and Leadership and the College of Education at The Ohio State University.

 **Patricia A. Alexander** is Professor and Distinguished Scholar–Teacher in the Department of Human Development at the University of Maryland. She has served as President of Division 15 (Educational Psychology) of the American Psychological Association, and as Vice-President of Division C (Learning and Instruction) of the American Educational Research Association. Since receiving her PhD from the University of Maryland in 1981, Dr. Alexander has published over 170 articles, books, or chapters in the areas of learning and instruction. She has also presented over 160 papers or invited addresses at national and international conferences. Currently, she serves as the editor of *Contemporary Educational Psychology* and *Instructional Science* and serves on 10 editorial boards, including those for *Reading Research Quarterly, Journal of Educational Psychology, Educational Psychologist, Journal of Experimental Child Psychology, Mathematical Thinking and Learning, Learning Disabilities Quarterly, American Educational Research Journal,* and the *Journal of Literacy Research.*

Among her many honors and awards, Dr. Alexander is a Fellow of the American Psychological Association and was a Spencer Fellow of the National Academy of Education. Recently, she was named one of the 10 most productive scholars in educational psychology and was the 2001 recipient of the Oscar S. Causey Award for outstanding contributions to literacy research from the National Reading Conference. In addition, she has received various national, university, and college awards for teaching.

1

Essential Components of Learning

Guiding Questions

- What can psychological theory and research contribute to our understanding of how students learn?
- What are the key dimensions of academic learning?
- How can instructional leaders apply the dimensions of learning?

What Can Psychological Theory and Research Contribute to Our Understanding of How Students Learn?

Innovation and reform are familiar threads in the fabric of education (Murphy & Alexander, 2002). Each new decade or political administration comes with new educational initiatives (e.g., *A Nation at Risk, Goals 2000, or No Child Left Behind*). Reformations, however, are also born from educational practice and research (e.g., teaching as scaffolding or cognitive apprenticing; Palinscar & Brown, 1984; Rogoff, 1990). Such initiatives serve to capture the prevailing philosophical orientations toward teaching practices of the time and signal developing trends in research and practices. Regrettably, these modifications to the educational landscape are often short-lived (Cuban, Usdan, & Hale, 2003). As a result, very few teaching or learning innovations that grow out of these initiatives are around long enough to produce broad and durable outcomes (Alexander, Murphy, & Woods, 1996).

For example, within the last 25 years, there have been several significant calls for educational reform. One of the first was the report of the National Commission on Excellence in Education, *A Nation at Risk*, which was published by the U.S. Department of Education (1983). The purpose of the report was to examine the state of America's schools. The overarching findings of the commission were that American schools and students were simply not succeeding. The Commission's fervent sentiments regarding these findings are captured by the following:

> If an unfriendly power had attempted to impose on America the mediocre educational performance that exists today, we might well have viewed it as an act of war. As it stands, we have allowed this to happen to ourselves. We have even squandered the gains in achievement made in the wake of the Sputnik challenge. Moreover, we have dismantled essential support systems which helped make those gains possible. We have, in effect, been committing an act of unthinking, unilateral educational disarmament. (National Commission of Excellence in Education, 1983, p. 5)

Within the report, the commission proposed several recommendations including: (a) strengthening graduation requirements so that all students establish a foundation in five *new* basics: English, mathematics, science, social studies, and computer science; (b) having schools and colleges adopt higher and measurable standards for academic performance; (c) significantly increasing the amount of time students spend engaged in learning; and (d) strengthening the teaching profession through higher standards for preparation and professional growth. What *A Nation at Risk* signaled was the entrance of the federal government into education reform in an unprecedented way.

Six years later, President George H. W. Bush hosted the 1989 Education Summit Conference in Charlottesville, Virginia, with the nation's 50 governors. The purpose of the summit was to discuss the issues and concerns highlighted in *A Nation at Risk* and set goals for American schools. The conference discussions resulted in the creation of eight educational goals to be achieved by the year 2000. These goals were signed into law by President Clinton in 1994 as the *Goals 2000: Educate America Act* (PL 103-227).

Specifically, it was proposed that by the year 2000: (a) all children in America will start school ready to learn; (b) high school graduation rates will increase to 90 percent; (c) students in grades 4, 8, and 12 will gain competency in the basic academic subjects; (d) the United States will rank first in the world in mathematics and science; (e) every adult American will be able to read; (f) every school in the United States will be free of drugs, violence, and firearms; (g) the nation's teaching force will have access to support and professional development; and (h) every school will promote partnerships that will increase parental involvement. In addition, *Goals 2000* established the National Education Standards and Improvement Council.

The most recent educational initiative is the *No Child Left Behind* Act (NCLB; PL 107-110), which was signed into law in 2001. The bipartisan act is based on four pillars, including stronger accountability; more freedom for states and communities; proven educational methods; and more educational choices for parents regarding their children. In establishing these pillars, the law requires that schools, districts, and states exhibit annual yearly progress in student achievement. To accomplish this feat, the government has also given states and local districts more authority in determining how best to spend federal education funds and has also begun to establish numerous federal grant programs to support school-based educational research. The primary requirement of all of these grant programs is that the awards must go to support scientific, predominantly quantitative research on educational interventions, or research that will lead to successful educational interventions.

What has been noticeably absent across all these potential reform initiatives, however, are the insights and understandings contained within the vast bodies of psychological research on teaching and learning that have been conducted over the last 100 years. Essentially, educational and psychological researchers have played little, if any, role in the creation of these national reform initiatives. It was just such a perspective that provided the impetus for Charles Spielberger, President of the American Psychological Association (APA), to call on the psychological research community in 1990 to assume more responsibility for improved education for all learners by taking a stronger and more active role in educational reform. Like William James (1890) before him, Spielberger believed that the accumulated knowledge base in psychology should, in theory, prove invaluable to educators and to those in the political and public realms. Yet in practice, the collective wisdom of psychology had exerted only limited influence in educational reform and everyday instructional practice (Spielberger, 1998), due in part to psychology's failure to make its findings accessible and pertinent.

What Are the Key Dimensions of Academic Learning?

In response to Spielberger's call for a greater and more meaningful presence for psychological theory and research in educational initiatives and reforms, the American Psychological Association formed a Presidential Task Force on Psychology in Education. This task force was composed of renowned educational theorists and researchers whose mission was to distill the 100-plus years of psychological findings into statements of principle that could guide the reformation of American schools.

This mission of the task force (i.e., to formulate core, evidence-based principles that could effectively guide educational reform and practice) was clearly daunting and required years of dedicated effort. At its conclusion, the final report of the task force listed 14 core principles for school reform, covering a number of areas of learning, instruction, and assessment. (For more information, see the 1997 summary report of the Work Group of the American Psychological Association's Board of Educational Affairs, at www.apa.org/ed/lcp.html.)

As a step in validating those 14 statements of principle, we were asked by the task force to conduct an exhaustive search of the relevant psychological and educational literature for studies that substantiated the initial draft of those principles. The results of that search (Alexander & Murphy, 1998b), which contributed to the revision and finalization of the principles, pinpointed five broad dimensions of theory and research that were the foundations of the learner-centered principles. Among those five dimensions were development (i.e., orderly and systematic changes that occur as a result of time and experience) and the knowledge base (i.e., one's stores of understandings and conceptions about everything); motivation/affect (i.e., a state that energizes and directs behavior); and strategic processing and executive functioning (i.e., the ability to reflect upon and regulate one's thoughts and behaviors). In addition, the original five dimensions of learning included a dimension called situation/context. This dimension referred to various environmental factors, such as ability grouping, and sociocultural factors, such as low socioeconomic status, that influence student learning in classrooms. Given the brief nature of this volume, we were forced to narrow our focus pertaining to situation/context. Specifically, we chose to focus on shared learning in classrooms, because we felt that social interaction and shared learning are at the heart of student learning in classrooms. Together, these five dimensions of learning form the backbone for this volume.

Our purpose here is to focus on the five dimensions and to further distill each into guiding educational principles that can aid instructional leaders in their efforts to create effective learning environments that culminate in academic excellence for all students (see Table 1.1). As we begin the discussion of psychology's potential contributions to student learning and achievement, we must acknowledge that the sheer magnitude of topics, questions, and actions we *could* address is overwhelming and well beyond the scope of this volume. While the selection of the five key dimensions of learning was a first step in managing this effort, an additional step was required to narrow our scope even further.

Specifically, we turned to focus groups of educational researchers and instructional leaders and listened to the specific questions and concerns they voiced for each of the key areas (cf. Alexander, 2005). From those focus group discussions, we selected several central and recurring questions to guide us. These questions formed the basis for Chapters 2 through 6 (see Table 1.1).

It is important to us that those framing questions came from *real* educational leaders trying to understand how psychology and education can come together to enhance learning for all students. In addition, the responses to those questions grew out of the research literature in educational psychology and related disciplines (e.g., development, motivation, and policy). We wanted to ensure that school administrators acting on these principles could operate with confidence that the ideas they represent are more than one's hopes, conjectures, or opinions, and are, in fact, evidence-based principles.

How Can Instructional Leaders Apply the Dimensions of Learning?

We have chosen to cast these guidelines in the form of principles for practice because we want to ensure that school leaders have the freedom to personalize and apply them in ways that are well suited to the situation and context in which they operate (see Table 1.1). We want to honor the knowledge and abilities of school administrators by allowing them to breathe life into the principles we have identified. Specifically, in Chapter 2, we explore the typical milestones that students will experience as they advance through school. In addition, we discuss what these milestones mean for administrators and teachers and how they can work to promote optimal learning environments in light of these milestones. What is clearly established in the literature is that human learning and growth is a continuous interchange between the generalizable, predictable patterns on the one hand, and individual differences in human behaviors and characteristics on the other.

Educators must be knowledgeable about common benchmarks of human development, regardless of whether the focus is on cognitive, socioemotional, or moral domains (e.g., Case, 1993; Kohlberg, 1981). Although not all these patterns are age-specific, teachers should be informed about the typical developmental levels expected for a particular age or grade. By knowing and understanding these various patterns, instructional leaders can plan professional development for teachers pertaining to developmentally appropriate activities and tasks that challenge students and enhance individual and group learning.

The influence of living in an information age will come to the forefront in the chapter on knowledge (Chapter 3). In this chapter, we will explore what it means to know something and consider various principles for effective teaching. For example, one's prior knowledge is an extremely strong force that directs students' attention; colors their judgments about what is relevant or important; impacts their comprehension and memory; and shapes the way they perceive their world (e.g., Reynolds & Shirey, 1988). A student's prior experiences, beliefs, and knowledge serve as the scaffold that supports the construction of future knowledge.

We will also discuss misconceptions and the question of why we form erroneous or naïve ideas that remain highly resistant to change, even in the face of powerful evidence. We will offer some strategies that instructional leaders can help teachers employ to challenge students' erroneous, misleading, and sometimes damaging concepts or attitudes, so that students can progress in their learning and achievement. Toward this goal, we examine how aspects of the learning task, instructional materials—as well as characteristics of the learners themselves—all contribute to the formation or deconstruction of such naïve conceptions.

When it comes to the areas of motivation and affect (Chapter 4), we will look closely at learners' academic goals and competency beliefs (i.e., attributions and self-efficacy) and the contributions these make to subsequent successes and failures in school. Here we will address questions that trouble many instructional leaders, such as: What can be done with a student who has lost any belief in his or her ability to succeed?, and Do external rewards help or hinder students' learning and development? As is evident to most instructional leaders, learning is altered by motivational and affective factors within the learner and in the learning environment. Indeed, the research on motivation and affect has documented that personal interest, intrinsic motivation, and internal commitment contribute to greater learning (e.g., Ames & Ames, 1989). That is, topics or areas of study for which students possess a deep-seated interest or are internally motivated to pursue will likely relate to higher achievement. Similarly, those learners who have goals of pursuing understanding (i.e., mastery or learning goals) rather than performing for external rewards or recognition are more apt to achieve in school (e.g., Murphy & Alexander, 2000). In particular, when students set their sights on learning for its own sake—rather than to gain acclaim or rewards—they are more apt to achieve competence (Alexander, 1997b). In our discussion, we will offer techniques that can make the content of instruction truly relevant and valuable to students.

The chapter on strategic processing and problem solving (Chapter 5) brings additional theory and research to bear on education and student learning. First, we will distinguish between skillful and strategic behavior and ponder the role each plays in learning and development. We will also discuss a range of strategies that can be applied to an array of problems. Some of these strategies have more general and broader use than others, whereas other strategies are closely linked to certain subjects or particular tasks. Likewise, some strategies are rather traditional, including those employed by the ancients to retain their cultural legacy. However, we also overview novel or less prototypical strategies that seem particularly relevant for living and learning in this informational and technological age, such as identifying and navigating sources.

To assume that one can simply have students memorize and routinely execute a set of strategies is to misconceive the nature of strategic processing or executive control. Such rote applications of these procedures represent, in essence, a *nonstrategic* approach to strategic processing. It has become increasingly clear, as well, that strategic processing or executive control is not only a purposeful undertaking but also an effortful one (Borkowski, Carr, & Pressley, 1987). This means that it is difficult to bring about changes in students' strategic processing without addressing issues of motivation, interest, and self-regulation (Alexander, 1997b). In this chapter, we offer principles to help make strategic processing an explicit and valued component in instruction, and mechanisms for orchestrating and maintaining a challenging but supportive learning environment. Such efforts should translate into greater learning gains for students.

In Chapter 6, the issue of learner differences arises again in our investigation of theory and research on social learning, with particular attention to the role of situation and context. We will touch on the role of human and nonhuman resources in creating an effective learning environment, as a means of recognizing how such resources can alter the course of learning and teaching.

One outcome of this growing body of research is the understanding that the learning context and the role of the teacher as the facilitator and guide of these social exchanges is vital (Radziszewska & Rogoff, 1988). In essence, performance is enhanced when learners are able to benefit from the guidance of a knowledgeable adult (e.g., a teacher) who promoted their exploration and interchange. As the learner develops in an area or in relation to a given task, then the level of assistance provided by the teacher should decrease proportionately (e.g., Brown & Palincsar, 1989). This lessening of external direction and support from a teacher or adult should theoretically contribute to more independent functioning on the part of the student and, likewise, enhance the possibility that transfer of the acquired knowledge or skill will occur both in and out of class. Essentially, the primary goal of this chapter is to contemplate techniques, such as cooperative, shared learning, or discussion approaches, that build positively on the cognitive, motivational, and cultural differences that exist within the classroom community.

Finally, in Chapter 7, we again highlight the important role that psychological research can play in everyday educational practice. Moreover, we emphasize the interactive nature of the five dimensions of learning. Although the five dimensions of learning are discussed in separate chapters in this volume, it is important to recognize and embrace their interrelations to promote optimal learning. Theoretically, we can extract cognition from affect, knowledge from strategic processing, or social influences from development, but these dimensions of learning remain inextricably intertwined in the real world. For example, knowledge and motivation are very closely related and influence one another during learning (Alexander 1997a). In essence, the more knowledge students possess about frogs, the more likely they are to become interested in frogs (e.g., Schiefele, 1991). Similarly, strategic processing is correlated with one's motivational or affective state (e.g., Hidi & Anderson, 1992). Thus, whether students can tackle complex mathematics problems—or make sense of demanding chapters in their science textbooks—depends not only on whether they have acquired critical problem-solving or comprehension strategies but also on whether they have the will or desire to engage in such effortful processing. Further, development is strongly tied to factors pertaining to situation and context (e.g., Ogbu, 1974; Scarr, 1992). For instance, how well students can perform on aptitude and intelligence tests, which are considered indicators of their cognitive development, is reflective of the learning opportunities they have had or the resources that have been made available to them during their formative years.

In light of the interdependence of these dimensions of learning, educators have a greater chance to make significant and long-term changes by approaching learning in a systemic fashion (Salomon, 1991). In his analysis of human behavior and the experiences from which it arises, Dewey (1930) expressed this precept with the words: "[N]o act can be understood apart from the series to which it belongs" (p. 412). We could not agree more. Moreover, as this volume will demonstrate, there is extensive research that upholds the important roles that the knowledge base; strategic processing or executive control; motivation and affect; development and individual differences; and situation or context play in promoting optimal student learning. However, the interrelatedness of these dimensions of learning is also a reminder that educators cannot focus solely on one aspect of student learning (e.g., strategic processing) and expect that maximal development will result. Rather, the message is clear that optimal student learning and development are predicated on the continual attention to all these dimensions for all learners. There is simply no shortcut.

Table 1.1 Overview of the Dimensions of Learning, Guiding Questions, and Educational Implications

Dimensions of Learning	Guiding Questions	Educational Implications
	Development	
Learning, ultimately a unique adventure for all, progresses through various common stages of development influenced by both inherited and experiential/environmental factors.	What is development? What are the developmental milestones for preschool to high-school students? How do instructional leaders put development research into practice?	*Early Childhood* • Ensure safety and security. • Create symbolic richness. • Encourage physical and cognitive engagement. • Expose children to enticing and varied experiences. • Operate on simple and clear rules for social interaction. • Support self-exploration and choice. • Use play as an opportunity for learning and self-expression. *Preadolescence* • Afford opportunities for extended exploration of topics and domains. • Focus problem solving around personally relevant problems. • Provide opportunities for specialized physical activities. • Encourage cooperative and shared learning activities. • Encourage students to consider issues from multiple perspectives.

Dimensions of Learning	Guiding Questions	Educational Implications
		• Require support for decisions and opinions.
		• Stimulate strategic thinking and self-evaluation.
		Adolescence
		• Encourage the pursuit of individual interests.
		• Expose students to varied career fields.
		• Promote individualization and creative processing.
		• Involve students in decision making.
		• Build on social interactions and peer relations.
		• Introduce complex, abstract problems and content.
		• Support students' social involvement and activism.

The Knowledge Base

Dimensions of Learning	Guiding Questions	Educational Implications
One's existing knowledge serves as the foundation of all future learning by guiding organization and representations, by serving as a basis of association with new information, and by coloring and filtering all new experiences.	What is knowledge? How do students acquire or alter their knowledge? How do instructional leaders put knowledge research into practice?	• Students' understandings, beliefs, and interests, rather than those of the teacher or curriculum supervisor, must be the central starting point for meaningful instruction. • Administrators and teachers must ensure that high-quality oral and written texts are used in schools and classrooms.

(Continued)

Table 1.1 (Continued)

- Administrators and teachers should present themselves as but one credible source of information in the school and classroom.
- Teach students how to frame sound arguments and provide support for their assertions.
- Administrators and teachers need to function as models of reflection, analysis, and argumentation.

Motivation and Affect		
Motivation or affective factors, such as intrinsic motivation, personal goals, attributions for learning, and self-efficacy, along with the motivational characteristics of learning tasks, play a significant role in the learning process.	What does it mean to be motivated? How do students' goals and competency beliefs relate to their learning and achievement? What can instructional leaders do to foster motivation in students?	<ul><li>Make motivation a primary focus in the learning environment.</li><li>Build on students' existing needs, drives, goals, and personal interests.</li><li>Challenge students' minds in meaningful ways.</li><li>Acknowledge students' efforts and accomplishments appropriately.</li><li>Maintain high expectations for all students.</li><li>Use feedback that highlights student effort and control.</li><li>Conceptualize motivation as a continuous, multifaceted, and developing process.</li></ul>

Strategic Processing		
The ability to reflect upon and regulate one's thoughts and behaviors is essential to learning and development.	What does it mean to be a strategic learner? Are some basic strategies required to achieve academically? What principles can instructional leaders employ to promote students' strategic behavior?	• Strategic thinking must be demonstrated and modeled. • Strategic thinking must be paired with explicit instruction. • Integrate strategy instruction with content in ways that are meaningful and practical. • Strategic competence begins with just a few strategies. • Students' strategic effort must be prompted, scaffolded, and rewarded. • Encourage the self in strategic thinking, such as goals, personalization, self-regulation, and self-assessment.
Shared Learning		
Learning is as much a socially shared undertaking as it is an individually constructed enterprise.	What is meant by shared learning? Are there approaches to shared learning that promote achievement? How can instructional leaders promote shared learning in classrooms?	• Social interaction patterns must match instructional goals. • Judgments about socially shared practices should be based on valid and reliable evidence. • Be sure that the configuration and consistency of the group work for the students.

2

Growth and Development Stages in Grades PreK–12

Guiding Questions

- What is development?
- What are the developmental milestones for preschool to high-school students?
- How do instructional leaders put development research into practice?

What Is Development?

Development is about change—systematic and predictable change. The study of development is one of the oldest and most fertile branches of psychology. The goal of development is to understand the significant and complex transformations that humans undergo from womb to tomb (see Table 2.1). Think for a moment about how much you have changed in your life. Obviously, your body has grown and changed since you were born, but so has the way you think and reason, the way you feel, and the ways you see and relate to others.

Table 2.1   Definitions of Relevant Terms

Term	Definition	Example
Cognitive Development	How our minds and mental processes change over time.	*Teachers in the primary grades must be equipped with a number of techniques to help students learn to read both at the beginning and the end of the year after their mental processes have developed.*
Developmental Milestones	Markers of noticeable change that should be evident as children mature physically, cognitively, socially, and emotionally.	*Because middle-school children are more developed physically, cognitively, and socially, teachers are able to plan more cooperative activities for them than they would be able to for younger students.*
Physical Development	How our bodies and their functioning change over time.	*Elementary teachers must be cautious of the physical activities they plan for their classes; while they may be the same age, not all students are in the same stages of physical development and may not be able to complete the same activities.*
Socioemotional Development	How our concept of ourselves, our relationships with others, and our emotions develop.	*While 1st-grade students may relate to teachers and administrators as parental figures, 5th-grade students do not, because they have become more mature.*

Development often categorizes the changes humans experience into three major domains: physical, cognitive, and socioemotional. Physical development refers to how our bodies and the functioning of our bodies change over time. *Physical development* addresses such topics as motor development and health-related issues (Tanner, 1990). *Cognitive development* covers how our minds and mental processes change over time (Byrnes, 2001). *Socioemotional development* concerns how our concept of ourselves, our relationships with others, and our emotions develop (Erikson, 1963).

Despite the existence of these three categories, it is important to remember that the physical, the cognitive, and the socioemotional aspects typically work together. Each area influences the others (Berk, 1999). Development provides administrators and teachers with information essential to understanding their students. For example, development offers a detailed picture of what physical, cognitive, and socioemotional traits are typical for individuals at particular ages or stages of development. It also helps school professionals understand the range of differences they might encounter at a particular age. With such information, teachers can more successfully implement a curriculum, and they can more effectively evaluate student performance. Moreover, with developmental knowledge, teachers can better determine how instructional methods should be adapted to meet the needs of all students in their schools and classrooms. With this knowledge, administrators will be able to provide grade-specific professional development for their teachers based upon the needs and capabilities of students they teach. Further, administrators should be better able to advise teachers on how to deal more effectively with the behavioral problems faced in their classrooms.

What Are the Developmental Milestones for Preschool to High-School Students?

Milestones are markers placed along a road or trail that let us know how far we have come in a journey. *Developmental milestones* serve much the same purpose. They are markers of noticeable change that should be evident as children mature physically, cognitively, socially, and emotionally. These developmental milestones can help administrators and teachers plan each phase of students' developmental journey by assisting them in orchestrating appropriate learning environments that correspond to students' developmental strengths and needs.

Developmental milestones serve us best when they describe the whole learner. Examining only students' physical attributes, cognitive characteristics, or socioemotional patterns is not enough. Students' success in schools is dependent on the interactions of these dimensions. Therefore, we weave together physical, cognitive, and socioemotional characteristics of learners at three educational levels—early childhood, middle school, and high school—as a way of creating developmental profiles of preK–12th-grade students.

Early Childhood Education: A Period of Exploration

For many young children, the first years in school are an exciting time of personal exploration (Alexander, 2005; White & Coleman, 2000). Indeed, the confluence of physical maturation, improved motor skills, increased cognitive abilities, and expanding social horizons sets the stage for a promising period of learning (Cowan, 1995). More than at any other period of schooling, the early childhood years set

Figure 2.1   Identifying Developmental Milestones

Development Trends in an Educational Context		
	Physical	*Cognitive*	*Socioemotional*
Early Childhood	Increases in height and weight proceed at a slow pace until adolescence. Body proportions become more similar to those of adults. Increasing fine motor abilities such as those needed for drawing and writing. Gross motor processes like those used in skipping, jumping, or dancing become more coordinated. Increases in physical speed and endurance.	Symbolic thinking enhanced, allowing for linguistic and mathematical learning. Concept formation aided by the ability to think categorically. Improved attention and memory. Can solve simple problems with concrete aids, such as adding or subtracting with toy counters. Has expanding vocabulary and uses more complex language structures. Grasps distinctions between real/pretend. Explores social relations through play.	Explores independence and emerging role through make-believe and self-initiated tasks. Expands social relations. New tasks and shared experiences may promote feelings of industry and desire for success. Egocentricism in moral reasoning with concern for rewards/punishments or self-satisfaction.
Middle School	Increased coordination in gross and fine motor processes. Faster reaction times. Initial pursuit of domain-specific motor tasks such as those used in organized sports (e.g., soccer) or specialized physical activities (e.g., dance). Initiation of growth spurt and onset of puberty in some females. Reach 70 to 90 percent of adult height.	Improvement in logical thought. Increased ability to use multiple problem-solving strategies at once. Base of background knowledge expanded. Increased ability to self-monitor and self-regulate. Able to modify language to fit audience and to learn through verbal exchanges. May show evidence of emerging formal operational thought.	Increased need for industry as they face more diverse and complex tasks. Demand for social interaction and cooperation increases. Moral reasoning tends to fall in the conventional level, where actions are shaped by compliance to moral codes. Actions judged as right or wrong.
High School	Physical growth spurt and puberty likely ongoing in males but concluded in females. Increased muscle mass in males. Increased fat cells in females. Heightened pursuit of domain-specific motor and physical activities. Greater concern for appearance. Rise in sexual drive.	Can think and solve problems of an abstract/hypothetical nature. Able to consider long-range consequences. Capable of weighing problems from multiple perspectives. Displays complex language patterns. Can see relationships among seemingly diverse concepts. Can be novel or creative in thinking. Capable of self-regulation.	Sphere of social influences expands. Questions about the future arise. A sense of self begins to take shape. Issues of intimacy may arise. Moral reasoning for most still based on compliance with conventional codes. A few may judge right and wrong on the basis of abstract principles of justice and fairness.

the foundation for subsequent learning (Whitehurst & Lonigan, 1998). These first years of formal schooling are what Rousseau (1762) and others (U.S. Department of Health and Human Services, 1994) would describe as the most critical period in children's formal learning.

By the time young children first experience formal learning, they have typically developed enough trust in caregivers and gained sufficient control of their own bodies to venture from the security of home (Erikson, 1963). Further, the ability to think symbolically allows these young minds to participate in linguistic and mathematical learning that would have been beyond their abilities years before (Piaget, 1955).

Of course, the essential learning tools of these young students remain their senses. Young children learn best when they are both mentally and physically engaged (Rubin, Fein, & Vandenberg, 1983). Improved coordination of fine and gross motor abilities also supports children's physical and mental engagement (Roberton, 1984; Tanner, 1990). For instance, they are now able to manipulate small implements like pencils, crayons, or scissors (fine motor), and they are also able to jump, skip, and run in a coordinated manner (gross motor).

Because of these increased physical and mental abilities, the world of print opens up to these young children. With the ability to read come untold avenues for exploration (Adams, Treiman, & Pressley, 1998; Juel, 1988). Similarly, because these young children can now make sense of numeric symbols, they are able to perform simple mathematical tasks like counting, adding, and subtracting (English, 1997). When these newly formed abilities are combined with increasing attention spans, improved memories, and the ability to distinguish the real from the imagined, young children are primed for significant academic exploration (Astington, 1993; Wellman & Gelman, 1998).

Thankfully, most children in kindergarten and 1st-grade exhibit an honest excitement for learning and an enthusiasm for exploration (Paris & Cunningham, 1996). Because children at this age are still rather self-centered and limited in their abilities to interact socially, the early childhood years are also periods of social experimentation (Munuchin & Shapiro, 1983). Children in kindergarten and 1st grade must learn how to function within a large social unit. This means they must learn how to meet their own needs in a socially appropriate way. They must also learn how to follow simple social conventions necessary for maintaining order in a classroom (Kohlberg, 1976), like waiting their turn to speak or participate in a class activity.

Middle School: The Period of Expansion

While early childhood education builds a solid foundation for development, the middle-school years are about expansion (Alexander, 2005). During these preadolescent years, when children's physical, cognitive, and socioemotional capabilities continue to grow and improve, education broadens and deepens their existing knowledge and skills.

Preadolescent students have passed some developmental hurdles (Kohlberg, 1981; Piaget, 1955). Their bodies have become stronger, more proportioned, and their movements faster and more coordinated. In fact, most have reached 70 to 90 percent of their adult height by the end of middle school. Toward the conclusion of this preadolescent period, some females experience growth spurts and the onset of puberty (Tanner, 1990). Also, during this period, many children find satisfaction in some form of specialized physical activity such as baseball, soccer, dance, or gymnastics (Seifert, Hoffnung, & Hoffnung, 1997).

In addition, middle-school students are able to see the world without the egocentric blinders that constrain everything younger children do and say (Damon & Hart, 1988). They are also faced with more diverse, subject-specific, and complex school tasks than younger students (Erikson, 1980). This results in greater need for personal industry and an increased chance of academic frustration. Perhaps this is one reason why student motivation declines during the middle-school years (Wigfield, Eccles, & Pintrich, 1996). Through their explorations and ongoing experiences, these children's background knowledge and conceptual understanding expand (Sigelman & Shaffer, 1995).

Even though a few preadolescent students may show evidence of emerging formal operational thought, most are concrete operational thinkers (Inhelder & Piaget, 1958). This means that they can think logically and use multiple strategies simultaneously, which makes them better equipped to solve or reason through an array of academic problems. Moreover, when problems are personally relevant and include concrete referents, these children's mental abilities are even more efficient and effective (Alexander et al., 1989). Preadolescents can also display an ability to self-regulate their performance (Flavell, Miller, & Miller, 1993).

Interactions with others become more important during middle school (Wentzel, 1999). These interchanges are helped by preadolescents' ability to modify their language to suit their audience (Deutsch & Pechmann, 1982). They can also listen and react to the ideas of others, which allows them to gain from social exchanges. However, as conventional moral reasoners, they still tend to see the world in terms of right and wrong or black and white, as defined by established moral and behavioral codes (Kohlberg, 1981).

Secondary School: The Period of Experimentation

Most adolescents define their identities (e.g., "Who am I?") and consider the person they are becoming (e.g., "Who will I be?") during the high-school years. In high school, immediate and pressing needs clash with concerns for the future. Thus adolescence is, in many ways, a time for physical, cognitive, and socioemotional experimentation under the watchful and caring gaze of knowledgeable adults (Alexander, 2005).

Adolescence is a period of physical, cognitive, and socioemotional transformation and upheaval (Sigelman & Shaffer, 1995). Teenage males are often in the throes of growth spurts and puberty, while females, who have likely completed much of this transformation, are confronting their heightened feelings of sexuality (Tanner, 1991). As bodies mature, muscle mass among males and fat cells among females increase. Concern for appearance and attractiveness is also evident in this period, particularly among females (Pesa, 1999). In addition, increasing numbers of adolescents confront issues of intimacy and become sexually active. In fact, about 50 percent of the females between 15 and 19 have engaged in sexual intercourse (Zuckerman, 1999).

Adolescence also brings significant cognitive changes. Some high-school students move into formal operational thought, while their peers remain concrete and linear in thinking (Piaget, 1930). Those in formal operations can solve complex, abstract, and hypothetical problems. In addition, these mature thinkers can consider the long-range consequences of actions, weigh multiple perspectives simultaneously, and ponder future possibilities.

Other factors aid these students' reasoning and analysis. They are capable of complex language use in oral and written communication, and they can apply their linguistic skills in their expanding social circles (Piaget, 1955). In addition, adolescents can grasp relations among seemingly diverse concepts and can devise their own novel or creative solutions to problems (Piaget, Montanegro, & Billeter, 1977). Even though moral reasoning for most adolescents is still based on compliance with conventional codes, a few teenagers may differentiate right and wrong on the basis of abstract principles, such as justice and fairness (Kohlberg, 1981).

How Do Instructional Leaders Put Development Research Into Practice?

With the developmental milestones pinpointed for preK–12th-grade students, and their physical, cognitive, and socioemotional profiles outlined, we consider what administrators and teachers can do with this developmental knowledge to promote students' academic achievement.

Effective Learning Environments for Early Childhood Students

To promote optimal learning, teachers need to create learning environments that complement young children's physical, cognitive, and socioemotional characteristics (Bredekamp, 1987) with support from the school's administrators. As such, those responsible for creating effective learning environments at the early childhood level should consider the following pedagogical principles.

Ensure Safety and Security

Because young children are widening their social circles and moving beyond familiar and comfortable territory (Munuchin & Shapiro, 1983), the classroom must be a secure and welcoming place. Young children must be able to put aside fears for their immediate well-being if they are going to see the learning environment as a place to explore and discover (White & Coleman, 2000).

Create Symbolic Richness

Young children's newly acquired ability to think symbolically remains fragile. Therefore, administrators must provide human and nonhuman resources to teachers so that they are able to encourage meaningful symbolic thinking by filling the environment with meaningful and enticing materials (Juel, 1988). The alphabet, common words, books, magazines, calendars, numbers, devices for weighing and measuring, and simple clocks are just a few of the materials that could be part of a learning environment rich in symbols (Morrow, 1997). As part of professional development, administrators should encourage teachers to frequently refer to these materials and promote students' interaction with them (Geary, 1994).

Figure 2.2 Attributes of Effective Learning Environments

Describing Environments That Benefit Learners		
Academic Level	Environmental Characteristics	Illustrative Case
Early Childhood Years	Ensure safety and security. Create symbolic richness. Encourage physical and cognitive engagement. Expose children to enticing and varied experiences. Operate on simple and clear rules for social interaction. Support exploration and choice. Use play as an opportunity for learning and self-expression.	Ms. Edwards's kindergarten class is lively and inviting. Samples of children's work are everywhere in the room, which is divided into several learning areas. At this time, three children are playing at the home center, making a pretend dinner for their make-believe family. Four children are sitting at the center table with Ms. Edwards, who is working on their letters and sounds. A parent volunteer, Mrs. Taber, is at the art center with several children. They are making Valentine cards for their parents. Kennith and two classmates are busy building a "spaceship" in the big-blocks area of the room, while Molly and her best friends, Felecia and Seung-Bai, are playing a counting game in the back corner with the teacher's aide.
Middle-School Years	Afford opportunities for extended exploration of topics and domains. Focus problem solving around personally relevant problems. Provide opportunities for specialized physical activities. Encourage cooperative and shared learning activities. Encourage students to consider issues from multiple perspectives. Require support for decisions and opinions. Stimulate strategic thinking and self-evaluation.	Mr. Sperling has been a 4th-grade teacher for five years. Mr. Sperling thinks it is important for students to explore important topics deeply, so he ties aspects of the curriculum, such as mathematics, history, and science, together in thematic units. These thematic units stress hands-on problem solving. Right now, students are hard at work on the ecology unit. Some are looking up information on endangered species on the computer, while others are working on interview questions they are going to ask select community leaders. Mr. Sperling and the students discuss some of the projects they can pursue and also decide together how some of those projects will be evaluated.
High-School Years	Encourage the pursuit of individual interests. Expose students to varied career fields. Promote individualization, creativity, and self-determination. Involve students in decision making. Build on social interactions and peer relations. Introduce complex, abstract problems and content. Support students' social involvement and activism. Allow time for specialized physical and motor activities.	Jane Eisel's health class keeps students invested and engaged. Jane does not shy away from controversial and sensitive topics, like drug use and teen pregnancy. Nor does she believe in lecturing to these students. Instead, she allows them to consider various sides of the issues, provided that they can justify and support their positions with solid evidence. The students also must weigh the long-term effects of certain positive and negative behaviors. Jane also encourages her students to participate in socially valued activities. This past Thanksgiving, for instance, her class served meals at a homeless shelter. Some students volunteer as tutors for students with special learning needs. Much of the work in health class is done in groups, and students help determine their project grades.

Encourage Physical and Cognitive Engagement

Given that children still rely heavily on their senses to understand their world, the early childhood environment should be a place where mind and body are partners in learning (Rubin et al., 1983). Effective early childhood rooms should be filled with manipulative, hands-on objects and materials that can be stacked, counted, sorted, and compiled (Paris & Cunningham, 1996). For example, children can say "three," while counting three buttons and then writing down the number "3."

Expose Children to Enticing and Varied Experiences

The famous early childhood educator Maria Montessori (1964) understood the importance of enticing and varied experiences for developing young minds. Her ideas are still alive in effective early childhood classrooms (Cuffaro, 1991; Kostelnik, 1992; Maxim, 2003). Since the world cannot always come to these young children, effective administrators and teachers bring the world to them. Children might watch eggs hatch in a makeshift hatchery, look at leaves through magnifying glasses, or guess which objects will float or sink in a water basin. The classroom should become a place of exploring the world and learning from that exploration.

Operate on Simple and Clear Rules for Social Interaction

Because young children are still self-centered and not socially adept, they need guidance on how to interact with school personnel and classmates (Damon, 1983). Thus, effective early childhood classrooms operate around a few simple and clearly explained rules (e.g., "We share with our friends."). Children also need to be aware of the rewards and punishments that result from complying with or disobeying these community rules (Kohlberg, 1975). Since they are immature reasoners, these rewards and punishments help shape their social behavior.

Support Self-Exploration and Choice

Although young students need a predictable framework in which to learn and thrive, they still benefit from occasional self-exploration and choice (Paris & Cunningham, 1996). Some free play or open choice time should be commonly scheduled in early childhood classrooms. During this time, children can select the activities they pursue, and with whom. To maintain order, however, some teachers control the number of children who can play in any learning area (e.g., art center) at once. They may also encourage certain students to try new activities instead of staying with one or two favorites (White & Coleman, 2000).

Use Play as an Opportunity for Learning and Self-Expression

To young children, play is a wonderful arena for learning (Rubin et al., 1983). Through play, children use their minds in imaginative and creative ways. They not only problem-solve during play, but they also interact socially and physically with others (Pellegrini, 1988). In their play, young children try on different personas and act out particular roles. Teachers seeking to create effective early childhood environments can learn much about young children's development simply by watching and listening to them during play.

Effective Learning Environments for Preadolescent Students

In light of the physical, cognitive, and socioemotional milestones associated with the middle-school years, what do school administrators and their teachers need to consider when orchestrating meaningful learning environments? Based on the research, such effective learning environments should:

Afford Opportunities for Extended Exploration of Topics and Domains

Early childhood is about initial forays into learning. By comparison, middle-schoolers deepen their understandings of particular topics (e.g., endangered species) or academic subjects (e.g., social studies; Alexander, 1997b). Thus, effective middle-school administrators encourage their teachers to promote academic exploration by allowing them the time and resources for their students to investigate intriguing problems. Integrated units of study that bring together several content areas (e.g., history, mathematics, and reading) also allow for a richer and more principled pursuit of knowledge and skills (Harris & Alexander, 1998).

Focus Problem Solving Around Personally Relevant Problems

When middle-school administrators and teachers come together to plan curriculum and choose tasks and activities to reinforce students' understanding, they would be wise to target personally relevant problems (Bransford, Brown, & Cocking, 1999). Such problems permit students to use their own expanding base of background knowledge, give them a concrete focal point they need to think logically, and potentially raise their interest or motivation. In some cases, students can help choose the problem they investigate, which adds to their sense of ownership and the personal relevance of the task (Wigfield et al., 1996).

Provide Opportunities for Specialized Physical Activities

Cognitive pursuits are not the only areas that become more specialized during this period; so do physical and motor activities (Seifert et al., 1997). The physical developments that preadolescent students experience, combined with their increasing social abilities, make the middle-school period an opportune time to encourage students' interests in organized or specialized physical activities. Research suggests that involving students early in such regular physical activities puts them on the path to lifelong wellness (Walker, Sechrist, & Pender, 1987).

Encourage Cooperative and Shared Learning Activities

Because of their enhanced ability to communicate with others, preadolescent students profit from group learning experiences (Berk, 1999). Therefore, we often see greater use of cooperative and collaborative activities in middle-school classrooms. One benefit of these group learning approaches is that teachers do not always need to be the instructional guides (Webb & Palincsar, 1996). Students at this age can learn from one another. Thus, as we will discuss in detail in Chapter 6, cooperative and shared learning activities should be common tools in teachers' pedagogical repertoires.

Encourage Students to Consider Issues From Multiple Perspectives

Although middle-school students still think in rather concrete and sequential ways, they can weigh evidence from multiple perspectives (Piaget, 1955). Thus, middle school is an excellent time to explore multiple informational sources and even opposing sides of an issue. In fact, conceiving of lessons as cases of persuasion, where two sides of a problem are juxtaposed, can enhance understanding, increase interest, and foster the exploration of unquestioned ideas (see Chapter 3; Fives & Alexander, 2001).

Require Support for Decisions and Opinions

In order to improve student learning, effective middle-school administrators should encourage teachers in their curricular planning to include student support and justification of their decisions and opinions. Chambliss (with Murphy, 2002), for instance, has worked extensively with this age group and found that their thinking, discussion, and writing improve when they are taught the skills of argumentation and explanation. She teaches students how to identify a writer's or speaker's argument and then to judge whether that point has been well supported. Further, she helps students learn how to frame their own arguments or premises and to include evidence that justifies such statements. Beyond enhancing students' thinking abilities, these activities can provide a base for later formal operational thought (Inhelder & Piaget, 1958).

Stimulate Strategic Thinking and Self-Evaluation

Just as preadolescent students need guidance in learning how to ponder issues from multiple perspectives or how to frame and support an opinion, they need to be encouraged in their strategic processing (Pressley & McCormick, 1995). Strategies are procedures or techniques that aid performance or circumvent problems (Alexander, Graham, & Harris, 1998). Because of their importance to optimal learning and development, we devote an entire chapter to strategies (Chapter 5).

Teachers must recognize that strategic learning can be promoted by explicitly introducing various strategies to students and encouraging them to fit those procedures to the tasks at hand (Paris, Wasik, & Turner, 1991). Are students able to distinguish more important from less important information in what they read or hear, for example? What steps can teachers suggest for making such critical determinations? Concern for strategic thinking, including the ability to judge the quality of one's own work, needs to be evident in middle-school classrooms. Students should be encouraged to expand their strategic repertoire so they have the right mental tools for specific problems they will encounter (Paris et al., 1991).

Effective Learning Environments for Adolescent Students

On the basis of the physical, cognitive, and socioemotional characteristics of adolescents, we can put forward several recommendations for high-school administrators and teachers for creating environments that foster learning during this period. Specifically, effective environments for adolescent students should:

Encourage the Pursuit of Individual Interests

Experimentation involves pursuing individual or personal interests (Alexander, 1997a). By the time students reach high school, they hopefully have found curricular and extracurricular activities and topics in which they are personally invested. Effective high-school administrators support teachers in their efforts to discover students' personal interests and weave those interests into the school environment or into classroom tasks and discussions (Alexander & Jetton, 2000). Finding opportunities to combine students' individual interests with instructional goals can maintain students' engagement in the content and the learning process (see Chapter 4). It can also highlight the value of subject matter that might otherwise be treated with indifference. Also, personal interest may maintain students' pursuit of knowledge, even when problems are highly challenging (Alexander, 1997b).

Expose Students to Varied Career Fields

Secondary students are not just absorbed in the present. They are concerned about their futures. One critical question about the future pertains to career options (Ginzberg, 1972). In a few years, these students will be entering the workforce. They are more likely to make wise decisions about their futures if they are exposed to various careers. However, that exposure must be more than superficial, romanticized, and dramatized treatment of well-known occupations (e.g., doctor, lawyer, teacher, or nurse). Certainly, if students are making career decisions based on what they see on television, in movies, or in magazines, they will not understand what jobs are available and what they require (Ginzberg, 1972). Sadly, many high schools do an inadequate job of assisting students in this school-to-work transition, leaving students with fuzzy notions and unrealistic expectations (Grotevant, Cooper, & Kramer, 1986; Creed, Muller, & Patton, 2003).

Promote Individualization and Creative Processing

One of the advantages of formal operations is that students can think and act independently and creatively (Piaget et al., 1977). Adolescents are able to devise their own approaches to problem solving and make reasoned choices. Effective learning environments for these students encourage them to do just that. Rather than merely asking them to execute problems in the exact way they are taught, teachers should encourage high-school students to formulate their own tasks and solution techniques (Pressley & McCormick, 1995). Further, high-school teachers should be encouraged to give these students latitude in determining how these tasks or problems will be addressed and evaluated.

Involve Students in Decision Making

Administrators and teachers who work effectively with adolescents recognize that they must respect and appreciate these students and their abilities (Wigfield et al., 1996). Such respect and appreciation are evident when high-school administrators and teachers give students a voice in curricular decisions (Brown, Paulsen, & Higgins, 2003). Teachers at this educational level can solicit students' ideas and opinions on all facets of learning, including the criteria by which assignments or projects will be evaluated, and can include their ideas in curriculum planning meetings with administrators and peers.

For example, when requirements for awarding valedictorian were called into question, Mrs. Harvey, the high-school principal, and a committee of teachers and student leaders worked together to devise new criteria for this honor. Because of Mrs. Harvey's willingness to include the ideas of students in the new criteria, she also helped promote their skills in self-evaluation and enabled them to take ownership of the resulting criteria.

Such involvement promotes students' development of their self-regulation and self-monitoring abilities (Zimmerman, 1990). In addition, secondary-school teachers should give students the chance to judge their own work on the basis of those criteria and then compare their judgments against an accepted standard. Through such activities, students learn that their thoughts and views matter, as they gain skill in self-evaluation.

Build on Social Interactions and Peer Relations

Social interactions and peer relations are unquestionably a large part of an adolescent life (Erikson, 1980). Effective learning environments at the secondary level include group activities, class discussions, and peer learning that can tap into this social dynamic (Webb & Palincsar, 1996). Students can then learn from their classmates and not just from the teacher. Also, such arrangements can prove useful when students are at varying cognitive and moral stages of reasoning.

The ideas of concrete operational thinkers can be intermingled with those of students who reason at a more sophisticated and abstract level.

Introduce Complex, Abstract Problems and Content

The expanding minds of adolescent students make high school an excellent time to focus on problems and subject matter that are complex and abstract (Inhelder & Piaget, 1958). Although subjects such as algebra, physics, chemistry, political science, or philosophy are within the cognitive reach of some middle-school students, it is not until high school that many are ready for such demanding content. Thus, effective learning environments include ample content and problem-solving tasks that require students to use their newly found capabilities for thinking abstractly (Piaget, 1930).

Support Students' Social Involvement and Activism

Whether students are at the highest level of moral reasoning or not, they should be encouraged to think beyond their own personal needs and wants (Gilligan, 1977). Encouraging students to consider larger social, cultural, and political issues can support these students' moral development (Kohlberg, 1975). Including discussions of broad and contentious social, cultural, and political issues in the curriculum can foster this learning process. It is also important to consider social and cultural differences when such issues are discussed (Shweder, Mahapatra, & Miller, 1990).

Chapter Reflections

Change is integral to the human experience and reflected in every part of our existence, from our physical makeup to the way we think, interact with others, and feel emotionally. Effective education requires an understanding of this fundamental change process. When we consider the various aspects of development, we become aware of the complexity that confronts students, administrators, and teachers daily. Thus, the developmental milestones we have outlined based on the rich theoretical and empirical literature on development can be invaluable tools to educators and educational leaders. These milestones mark the course of development that students are traveling and thus help administrators and teachers serve as more informed guides.

In this discussion, we looked closely at the physical, cognitive, and socioemotional milestones and ensuing characteristics for learners at three specific points in their schooling: early childhood years, middle school, and high school. We conceptualized early childhood as the period of exploration, a time when young children first venture into the new and exciting world of formal learning. In contrast, we portrayed middle school as a period of expansion, when students build on the foundation of knowledge and skills they established during early childhood. In high school, the developmental milestones involve experimentation as students not only deal with significant physical, cognitive, and socioemotional changes but also look ahead to their futures as adult members of society.

Thankfully, the richness of the developmental literature provides administrators and teachers with suggestions for orchestrating learning environments that complement the developmental profiles of their students. For instance, educators can furnish young children with stimulating and inviting experiences that feed their inherent curiosity and desire to learn. Likewise, administrators and teachers can encourage middle-school children to look more deeply and richly at the world around them and help those learners hone the tools they will require for independence and self-determination. Further, educators can help adolescents map their futures by identifying their unique abilities and interests and by encouraging these learners to make reasoned and thoughtful choices. All of this, however, requires school administrators and classroom teachers to recognize the milestones of student development and to take advantage of the information and guidance those milestones afford. The more educators and educational leaders know about development, and the more sensitive they are to the milestones that arise along the way, the more effective guides they can be for their students throughout this incredible journey into adulthood.

3

How Students Acquire Knowledge

Guiding Questions

- What is knowledge?
- How do students acquire or alter their knowledge?
- How do instructional leaders put knowledge research into practice?

What Is Knowledge?

There is no denying that individuals living in the 21st century are literally bombarded by information. Whether surfing the Internet or simply walking through the local shopping mall, it is a daunting task to know what to attend to and what to ignore. The same holds true for schooling. It seems that new curricular mandates and school textbooks have exponentially increased what students seemingly need to learn. Yet students' mental capacities have remained virtually unchanged over the centuries (Alexander et al., 1996). It would seem, therefore, that administrators and teachers have to help students learn "smarter," or more efficiently, so that they are not washed away in this continuous flood of information.

In this chapter, we will address the issue of building a knowledge base. In doing so, we begin by defining prior knowledge and then look more closely at particular states and forms of knowledge that play a role in effective teaching and learning. We also briefly address mechanisms for changing student knowledge, and close with guiding principles that administrators and teachers can use to help students build the principled knowledge that will carry them toward academic achievement.

Prior Knowledge

The term *prior knowledge* refers to the sum of what an individual knows (e.g., Alvermann, Smith, & Readence, 1985; Lipson, 1995). Thus, prior knowledge is synonymous with common terms like *background knowledge, experiential knowledge, world knowledge, preexisting knowledge,* and *personal knowledge.* Our prior knowledge encompasses all we know or believe, whether positive or negative, accurate or inaccurate, real or imagined, verifiable or nonverifiable (Alexander, 1998; Alexander, Schallert, & Hare, 1991). Every sound, smell, taste, or sight we encounter, whether it is part of "real" or "virtual" reality, has a chance of imprinting itself on our memories.

It is one sign of mental maturity that the boundaries between positive and negative, accuracy and inaccuracy, real and imagined, and verified and speculative become sharper. Thus, we can hear a scary story about monsters but recognize that such creatures are imaginary, in contrast to the two-year-old for whom monsters are real. The boundaries between verified and speculative or accurate and inaccurate are never completely delineated in our minds, regardless of our mental maturity or years of education. Rather, the life experiences that help us make these determinations are just one more aspect of our unique mental histories. In spite of the fact that our prior knowledge and experiences are as unique as our fingerprints, the life experiences we have in common with others can forge strong bonds and serve as powerful catalysts for subsequent communication and learning in schools (Bronfenbrenner, 1979).

The past three decades of research on prior knowledge have made it clear that our prior knowledge is continually at work, influencing how we see and interact with the world around us, whether we are conscious of that influence or not (Alexander & Murphy, 1998a). As such, it can be argued that no meaningful discussion of teaching and learning can take place without acknowledging the power of prior

Table 3.1   Definitions of Relevant Terms

Term	Definition	Example
Accretion Synonym: Assimilation	An elaboration or extension of existing knowledge structures that results from experiencing or acquiring new information.	*When an administrator shares the school policies with incoming teachers, the teachers readily absorb this new information into their existing knowledge structures about how the school operates.*
Conceptual Change	Transformations in a person's existing knowledge base that can range in magnitude from simple modifications to radical restructuring.	*When administrators adopt new instructional approaches for the school (e.g., reciprocal teaching), it is important that the teachers modify or change their conceptions of how to organize reading groups. The role of the administrator is to aid in this process of conceptual change.*
Ontology	Branch of philosophical study that pertains to views or beliefs about relations among things in and with the world.	*Some teachers hold to the view that competition is a beneficial approach to learning. That is, they believe that competition promotes academic achievement, when in fact it can actually thwart achievement.*
Radical Restructuring	Fundamental shift in knowledge.	*Many administrators were once students in schools where corporal punishment was acceptable. Over the years, they have drastically changed their perspective on this now frowned-upon practice.*
Tuning Synonyms: Accommodation, or Weak Restructuring	Form of conceptual change that requires that knowledge structure be adjusted or reformed to account for a new conceptual understanding.	*Administrators unfamiliar with new trends in teacher preparation may conceive of student teaching as a 14-week period of training in the school. As part of professional development schools, administrators would likely modify or tune their notion of the internship phase of preservice teacher development.*

knowledge. In essence, one cannot effectively teach without linking learning to students' existing thoughts, feelings, perceptions, interests, and beliefs (Alexander, 2000).

We also know that our mental histories are ever present. Students do not enter schools as blank slates, as Locke (1699) envisioned. In effect, our prior knowledge acts as the starting point for learning and the filter through which all that we see, hear, or feel comes to be understood. Therefore, it should come as no surprise that prior knowledge has been found to be a significant factor in many aspects of human learning and development.

Prior knowledge influences the degree to which individuals attend to (Reynolds & Shirey, 1988; Wade, 1992), understand, and remember what they see or hear (Anderson, Reynolds, Schallert, & Goetz, 1977). Similarly, prior knowledge influences the judgments people make as to what is relevant, accurate, or important (Alexander, Jetton, Kulikowich, & Woehler, 1994; Chinn & Brewer, 1993), as well as the mental representations they make about subsequent events or experiences (Cognition and Technology Group at Vanderbilt [CTGV], 1996). Prior knowledge also influences whether something is deemed interesting, credible, or persuasive (Murphy, 1998; Petty & Cacioppo, 1986) and the degree to which students are motivated (Eccles, Wigfield, & Schiefele, 1998; Pintrich & Schunk, 1996) and strategic in their behaviors relative to learning (Alexander & Judy, 1988; Alexander, et al., 1998).

Perhaps the most important aspect of prior knowledge, however, is the role it plays in future academic endeavors. Perhaps the single most substantive finding this century is that the knowledge that students bring to the learning task is the strongest predictor of what they will learn from that experience (Alexander, 1997b; Stanovich, 1986). The point is that prior knowledge will be either a formidable ally or foe for educators and educational leaders.

The States of Knowing

Prior knowledge is not, of course, a unitary construct. Rather, it is actually composed of various knowledges. Knowledge can be categorized in a number of different ways (e.g., state or type). Categorizing knowledge by state is particularly helpful to educators. This distinction bears on the way educators conceive their lessons, formulate their curricula, and construct their tests. Prior knowledge can exist in three states: *declarative, procedural,* and *conditional* (Alexander et al., 1991).

Table 3.2   Definitions of Selected Knowledge Constructs

Term	Definitional Statements
Conceptual Knowledge	Knowledge of ideas made up of content knowledge and discourse knowledge; comprised of what they are, how they function or operate, and the conditions under which they are used (Carey, 1985; Ryle, 1949).
Conditional Knowledge	Knowledge of when and where knowledge (declarative or procedural) could, or should, be applied (Alexander & Judy, 1988; Paris, Lipson, & Wixson, 1983).
Declarative Knowledge	Factual information; sometimes described as "knowing what" (e.g., Alexander & Judy, 1988; J. Anderson, 1983).
Discipline Knowledge	Highly formal subset of domain knowledge; knowledge of an academic subject; a specialized field or story, or particular branch of learning (e.g., Bazerman, 1981).
Domain Knowledge	More formal subset of content knowledge; a realm of knowledge that broadly encompasses a field of study or thought (e.g., Alexander & Judy, 1988; Glaser, 1984; Rabinowitz & Chi, 1987; Voss, Blais, Means, Greene, & Ahwesh, 1986). Synonyms: domain-specific, content-specific, or subject knowledge.
Explicit Knowledge	Knowledge that directly guides ongoing interactions with the world; analyzed knowledge; knowledge that is currently or usually the object of thought (Prawat, 1989).
Metacognitive Knowledge	Knowledge of knowledge; knowledge about one's cognition and the regulation of that cognition (Flavell, 1987; Garner, 1987).
Prior Knowledge	The sum of what an individual knows (e.g., Alvermann, Smith, & Readence, 1985; Lipson, 1983; Shuell, 1986). Synonyms: background knowledge, experiential knowledge, world knowledge, preexisting knowledge, and personal knowledge.
Procedural Knowledge	Knowledge one has of certain processes or routines; can be described as "knowing how" (J. Anderson, 1983; Ryle, 1949).
Self (Person) Knowledge	Knowledge of yourself as a thinker and learner (Flavell, 1985; Garner, 1987).
Sociocultural Knowledge	Attitudes and beliefs about the world and how to interact with it that arise from being a member of a particular social group or culture (e.g., Heath, 1983; Rosenblatt, 1978).
Strategic Knowledge	Knowledge of processes that are effortful, planful, and consciously invoked to facilitate the acquisition and utilization of knowledge (Alexander & Judy, 1988; Prawat, 1989).

(Continued)

Table 3.2 (Continued)

Term	Definitional Statements
Tacit Knowledge	Knowledge of which we are normally or currently not aware; unanalyzed knowledge (Prawat, 1989; Schön, 1988).
Task Knowledge	An understanding of the cognitive demands of a task (Doyle, 1983; Garner, 1987).
Topic Knowledge	The intersection between one's prior knowledge and the content of a specific passage or discourse (e.g., Freebody & Anderson, 1983; Hare & Borchardt, 1984).

SOURCE: Adapted from Alexander, P. A., Schallert, D. L., & Hare, V. C. (1991). Coming to terms with the terminology of knowledge. *Review of Educational Research, 61*, 315–343.

The three states of prior knowledge are somewhat analogous to the states of matter (e.g., solid, liquid, and gas). We were taught that water can be frozen into ice, melted into a liquid, or heated so much that it will become a vapor. Yet the basic chemical composition of water remains consistent, even as its appearance changes. In many ways, knowledge can undergo similar transformations and yet retain its basic composition. Further, students should be given many opportunities to encounter information in all its potential states.

Declarative Knowledge

Upon entering elementary school, parents often teach their children to recite their name and address in case they get lost. These kinds of specific facts, labels, definitions, explanations, or descriptions are referred to as declarative knowledge. Essentially, *declarative knowledge* pertains to the *thats* or *whats* of knowledge because it completes the response, "I know that . . ." (Ryle, 1949). This kind of knowledge is probably the most common form of knowledge taught in schools. Much like this book, the content that students study and the curriculum materials that educators process are frequently filled with such factual information. The value of declarative knowledge may be readily apparent to you. Without such knowledge, there would be no way to label, describe, or explain the world around us or to communicate those understandings to others.

The *thats* or *whats* students internalize as knowledge may exist as separate pieces or fragmented elements in memory, or they could be part of some integrated system of ideas on this topic (Byrnes, 1996).

Table 3.3 Comparing the Three States of Knowledge

	States of Knowledge		
	Declarative	*Procedural*	*Conditional*
Nature	Factual or *what* knowledge related to labeling, describing, or explaining.	Actions, routines, or *how* knowledge; concerned with demonstrating or performing.	Understandings dealing with *how, when,* or *why* declarative and procedural knowledge should be applied.
Teaching	Have students repeatedly define, explain, recall, and illustrate relevant terms and concepts.	Provide students with opportunities to engage in hands-on, repetitive practice of procedures or steps in a process.	Allow students to practice procedures under a variety of different conditions to determine when to use those procedures; prompt students to explain why, how, and for what reasons they made certain mental choices.
Evaluation	Recognition or recall of items, focusing on specific factual content; most useful in gauging the scope of students' knowledge of particular topics or domains. *Sample Item:* $6 \times 7 = \underline{\quad}$.	Performance-based assessments; demonstration activities; simulation tasks; focused on problem solving or decision making. *Sample Item: Executing a three-point turn during a driver's license test.*	Problem solving; creative or novel tasks; self-evaluative measures. *Sample Item: Playing a piece of music in the correct key signature.*

That is to say, they could be part of some well-formed concept. Concepts consist, in part, of such declarative knowledge pieces. Students who are new to a domain of study (i.e., acclimated or novices) have little declarative knowledge to draw on, and even this knowledge is often loosely configured in memory (Alexander, 1997b). The declarative knowledge of more competent learners, by comparison, is more central to the topic or domain at hand, more richly formed, and more tightly integrated. In other words, these competent students have more principled declarative knowledge.

Procedural Knowledge

Our vast store of prior knowledge is not limited to factual tidbits or to understandings that we can easily label or define. We also have knowledge that allows us to perform certain acts, such as moving pieces on a chessboard or fixing a leaky water pipe. Such understandings represent procedural knowledge. *Procedural knowledge* refers to the *hows* of our understanding (Ryle, 1949). This proceduralization of knowledge is critical to efficient and effective functioning inside and outside of classrooms.

You can appreciate the role of procedural knowledge in teaching and learning if you consider the number of actions or procedures in which you engage daily. When we are in the throes of acquiring some new procedure, the individual components or the declarative elements of the "thing" are much more evident to us. For example, before a medical student would ever be allowed to see patients, she would need a great deal of relevant declarative knowledge—from appropriate terminology (e.g., thoracic vertebrae or femur) to awareness of a host of medical conditions (e.g., psoriasis or scarlet fever). Over time, with continued exposure and practice, these separate elements begin to combine and fuse into action-related sequences, referred to as productions. Thus, our young doctor becomes increasingly familiar with the process linking particular symptoms with particular illnesses and conditions, as evidenced by her quick diagnosis of a given case.

With even more practice, these actions become almost second nature, or *automatic*. Certainly, most pediatricians can spot a cold virus from a mile away, despite a parent's insistence that his child has an infection. Once these procedures become highly automaticized, they can be executed with little mental effort. Even though it may be hard for you to imagine automaticity with respect to the medical profession, you certainly experience it in your everyday life.

Take learning to write a term paper as an example. Most of us have read term papers and may have even attempted to write term papers. We may know how to make an outline and create a concept map. We may even be very accomplished typists, and may write short stories well, but still lack the procedural knowledge to actually write a clear, effective term paper. As a novice, almost constant concentration is required on the basic elements of actually writing a paper—not the *thats* but the *hows*. It takes many hours of practice on the basic elements before there is any automaticity, and, for some individuals, writing a term paper will never be automatic.

Conditional Knowledge

Research in strategic processing and problem solving has also created an awareness of a third state of knowledge: conditional knowledge. Like procedural knowledge, conditional knowledge receives limited attention in educational practice, yet it is critically important in learning. Specifically, *conditional knowledge* deals with understanding *when, where,* and *for what reason* knowledge should be brought into play (Paris, Lipson, & Wixson, 1983). Unlike the production rules of procedural knowledge, those specified in conditional knowledge are not generally fixed. Instead, they are far more fluid and determined by factors in the immediate environment. As such, conditional knowledge requires that individuals evaluate the context and bring their declarative and procedural knowledge to bear as required by the conditions or circumstances.

To understand the significance of conditional knowledge, let us visit a hypothetical 9th-grade classroom where students are engaged in learning about the Supreme Court. By the conclusion of their Supreme Court project, these 9th graders could readily respond to questions testing their declarative knowledge of the characteristics of the judicial system. They could also conduct a mock trial that follows a script outlined by their teacher (procedural knowledge). Later in the school year, if the teacher confronts some significant disruptive behavior on the part of several students, the class might decide to use their acquired judicial knowledge of the law and legal procedures to conduct a review of their "accused" peers. In this instance, they will see how their new understanding of the judicial system can have value in the current situation. In order to do so, however, they must have the requisite conditional knowledge to know when, where, and under what circumstances the knowledge they have of the justice system can be brought to bear on the current class disruption (Alexander & Murphy, 1998b).

How Do Students Acquire or Alter Their Knowledge?

Learning is a process of acquiring, altering, and abandoning conceptions or understandings (Murphy & Mason, in press). This process of learning is the central focus of schooling (Woolfolk, 2001). In particular, one of the major goals of schooling is to examine our prior knowledge in light of scientifically held conceptions. Specifically, as students become more competent in subject matter domains (e.g., history or biology), we expect to see transformations in their knowledge base; that is, we expect to see *conceptual change* (Duit & Treagust, 2003). The concepts they know should become richer and more cohesive in structure, if learning is occurring, or these concepts may actually be transformed as a result of knowledge acquisition.

Knowledge Acquisition

At times, the new information we encounter fits easily within our existing knowledge structures, allowing those structures to expand without difficulty. For instance, when children learn more facts about their pets, they simply add this declarative information to their existing "pet" schema. This simple form of knowledge acquisition, called accretion (Rumelhart, 1980), accounts for the majority of our everyday learning and often goes unnoticed.

The process is similar for the acquisition of simple procedures. Generally speaking, what we expect of students as they become better educated in a field is more efficient and effective performance of key domain procedures. We expect students' procedures or scripts to become more automatic, more elaborate, and more efficient. William James (1890) described the automatization of particular routines as positive "habits of the mind." The catalyst for such automaticity would be continued practice or performance of those actions in rich contexts. James believed that if students could make the process of learning a habit of the mind, then education would become their friend for a lifetime. If, however, learning procedures fail to become habitual, then students must struggle educationally. Certainly, both types of students exist in schools.

As is true outside schools, learning experiences within schools do not always allow for the possibility of repeated performance of basic domain procedures. For example, not every student will get to focus the microscope or read a poem aloud to the class. There are educational barriers to forging these good "habits of mind." As is the case for fighter pilots or astronauts, schools simply cannot afford to hone students' skills in real-life situations. The cost in human and nonhuman resources would be too great. Similarly, it would not be reasonable or prudent for students to demonstrate their understanding of the judicial system by arguing a case in a real courtroom. However, technological advances have the potential to change these situations. Advances in hypermedia have allowed for rather sophisticated simulations of problem-solving or decision-making contexts (de Jong &

van Joolingen, 1998; Reimann & Schult, 1996). Learners at all stages of academic development can engage in meaningful practice that extends and reinforces their procedural, as well as declarative, knowledge.

Having acquired some declarative and some procedural knowledge, it is even more important that conditional knowledge be acquired. Fortunately, research suggests that learners who become increasingly more knowledgeable in a given area are simultaneously able to display cognitive flexibility, even as their actions become more automatic. The key seems to be that enhanced automaticity does not completely eliminate thought or reasoning. Our awareness of what we are doing lies very near the surface of consciousness, ready to be called into action at a moment's notice. In addition, because we are more practiced at what we are doing, we have more cognitive energy to allocate to related thoughts and actions. This increases the likelihood that we will perceive conditions that deepen our thoughts or enrich our actions.

Along with the *whats* and the *hows*, educators must provide opportunities to apply knowledge meaningfully under varying conditions. The more teachers help students understand the conditional or contextual dimensions that may exist in the performance of academic tasks, the more likely students are to use what they know effectively and efficiently. One way that teachers can help their students is to model the flexible use of knowledge under varying conditions. In doing so, teachers should explicitly discuss how and why they are using knowledge in a particular way under a given set of circumstances. By this action, students will be more likely to develop deeper and more meaningful understandings of the concepts being taught.

Altering Knowledge

Individuals begin to acquire knowledge as soon as they are able to mentally process information, and not all of that learning happens smoothly. At some point in our learning we encounter new pieces of related information or have an experience that conflicts with our prior knowledge. In such cases, our existing knowledge structures cannot simply incorporate the new insights or information. Instead, those structures must be moderately or even radically transformed. The processes required to make simple adjustments to our conceptual knowledge are quite different from those needed to reshape our understandings drastically. Researchers have identified three mechanisms for conceptual change that result in differing levels of mental transformation: accretion, tuning, and restructuring (Rumelhart, 1980).

As we discussed, the simplest and subtlest form of knowledge change is accretion. *Accretion* involves an elaboration or extension of existing knowledge structures resulting from experience or the acquisition of relevant information (Rumelhart, 1980). Accretion closely parallels Piaget's (1930) notion of assimilation. Despite its relative importance, accretion has not been the focus of much research. Instead, much of the research on altering knowledge has focused on troublesome notions and dramatic transformations. As such, the process of accretion is often downplayed in the literature. Despite accretion being overlooked, it is our perspective that administrators and teachers should understand that much of learning occurs through the process of accretion and that it is a fundamental mechanism for conceptual growth and development.

Let's use the idea of what "real" means to illustrate this mechanism of change. Lauren is a typical two year old who seems to equate being real with things in her environment that she can see, touch, hear, taste, or smell (i.e., anything she can sense). Among those things are people (e.g., mom or dad), animals (e.g., her dog Portia), and even the characters she sees on television (e.g., Elmo or Dora the Explorer). As she ages, Lauren's concept of "real" develops through accretion. She painlessly extends her understanding by incorporating her new babysitter, deer, and a new monster named Shrek into her existing knowledge categories.

Of course, not all knowledge acquisition goes so smoothly. In some situations, learning involves more than accumulating new facts, experiences, or relations. Sometimes our existing mental frameworks and models must be reshaped or adjusted in some manner to grow and develop conceptual understanding. In *tuning* (Rumelhart, 1980), *weak restructuring* (Carey, 1985), and *accommodation* (Piaget, 1930), the acquisition of conceptual understandings requires minor modifications to existing knowledge structures, which usually involves shifting or reordering categories or related attributes.

For example, if Lauren's parents are lucky they will be able to convince her that monsters are not real. In doing so, they may be able to avoid the need to continually reassure Lauren that no scary monsters are going to jump out of her closet and get her. The difficulty, however, is that the television provides sensory input that is quite real to Lauren. Such a shift will definitely require weak restructuring or tuning of her conceptual understandings. As Lauren gets older, her concept of "real" will likely take on new and more sophisticated dimensions, eliminating all cartoon characters from that category.

In some cases, which are probably the most rare form of change, new experiences or information result in profound reconstructions or changes that reflect an alteration in our fundamental world views (i.e., changes in causal relationships; Vosniadou, 1994). This fundamental shift in knowledge is generally referred to as *radical restructuring*. Many theorists believe that radical restructuring must be accompanied by theory or belief change that influences all the components of a concept (e.g., Carey, 1985; Vosniadou, 1994). In our example with Lauren, radical restructuring would require much more than accepting the notion that monsters are not real. Rather, Lauren would have to show evidence of completely restructuring her understanding of what it means to be real (i.e., existing in nature and in actual experiences). Simply moving monsters out of the category of real (i.e., tuning) would not be enough. It is difficult to know how to spark such radical restructuring during the course of regular instruction. The simple fact is that students are completely capable of holding two conceptually conflicting theories in their memories (Chinn & Brewer, 1993).

Although it may be surprising, the most dramatic form of conceptual restructuring seems to occur among experts (Alexander, 1997b; Perkins & Simmons, 1988). The knowledge of experts is so extensive and highly interrelated that a misconception can potentially infect much of what they know. Of course, the difficulty is that experts think they are correct, so abandoning or dramatically altering fundamental but erroneous notions is no small feat. Such change often requires the unraveling of much of what experts believe to be true about their fields. In other words, nothing short of a paradigmatic shift will permit experts to restructure their conceptions (Kuhn, 1970). From an administrator's perspective, such a transformation might involve a shift in the faculty's perception of teaching as knowledge transmission to a perception of teaching as the scaffolding of knowledge construction.

Understanding and Confronting
Sources of Resistance to Change

If you have ever tried to convince someone to change their mind about a particular issue, then you are familiar with the concept of resistance. Often, students' understandings are resistant to change. Moreover, it does not seem to matter whether the student is in the 2nd grade or studying in a doctoral program. As much of the research in teacher beliefs shows (Pajares, 1992), both educators and their students share sources of resistance to change. In essence, the life experiences of teachers and students seem to give individuals reasons for holding on to their naïve understandings in the face of contradictory evidence. What is also clear is that the process of altering conceptions is important for administrators and teachers alike. Simply put, administrators will likely need to change the conceptions of their faculty, and teachers will likely encounter students who possess entrenched, naïve beliefs instead of scientifically held conceptions.

Sources of Resistance

Chinn and Brewer (1993) set out to understand how students, at varying levels of proficiency, respond to data or conceptions that do not correspond to their existing understandings. Specifically, Chinn and Brewer were interested in students' responses to anomalous data. They posited that students' sources of resistance would shed light on how teachers could begin to influence these sources and actually accomplish conceptual change. They identified four categories of reasons given by people for resisting contradictory information. The first category was related to background or prior knowledge. Essentially, background knowledge seemed to infiltrate and govern many of the students' ideas, seemingly making it impossible to confront any erroneous concept that was part of their overall world view. Primitive beliefs about scientific concepts also made it difficult or impossible to see the merits of contradictory evidence or to think about and test new information in a scientific manner.

Second, students stated that the new alternative theory was not compelling and left room for alternative viewpoints, including their own. As such, students felt that it was not necessary to abandon their own personal theories. The third category Chinn and Brewer identified pertained to the quality of the anomalous data. If it is to be deemed acceptable, data should be compelling and come from multiple sources so that it can be verified or corroborated.

Finally, Chinn and Brewer found that students seemed to process the data at a superficial level rather than in depth. By so doing, there was actually no reason for students to abandon their old conceptions. In order for change to occur, the alternative data must be thoughtfully processed. In studying and articulating these categories of reasons for conceptual resistance, Chinn and Brewer (1993) hoped that teachers in classrooms could address these sources of resistance and made recommendations for counteracting all four sources of conceptual resistance.

Confronting Sources of Resistance

Chinn and Brewer (1993) felt that conceptual change was likely if teachers focused their instruction on the four potential sources of resistance they uncovered. In other words, they suggested that conceptual learning would be more likely if teachers explicitly attempted to influence students' prior knowledge and present them with a viable and compelling alternative. In addition, these researchers felt that it was particularly important that teachers offer students convincing evidence, and design learning environments and experiences that would promote deep processing of relevant information.

Influencing Prior Knowledge

Teachers often feel the pressure to cover a tremendous amount of content in classrooms. Interestingly, one of the things teachers usually do not address is students' prior conceptions (Chinn & Brewer, 1993). If it is assumed that the students' knowledge can be a source of their conceptual resistance, educators must focus directly on that knowledge.

Like Chinn and Brewer (1993), we suggest several ways that this can be accomplished. The first step seems to be to bring students' current understandings to the surface rather than allowing those ideas to stay mentally buried. For example, a teacher could use knowledge-cueing techniques like drawings, stories, or concept maps as mechanisms for bringing students' conceptualizations to the surface (Tekkaya, 2003). It is also important that students share their understandings with others (Murphy, Wilkinson, & Soter, 2004). By making their conceptions public, students are forced to solidify their positions. Requiring students to establish what they know appears to be an important step in the change process (Mason, 1996). Teachers can then use this information as a starting point for building subsequent knowledge.

In exploring students' prior knowledge, it may be important to have students discuss some questions that seem to be more fundamental and ontological in nature. *Ontology* is branch of philosophical study that pertains to views or beliefs about relations among things in and with the world. For example, a middle-school teacher might find it worthwhile to do a lesson on single-celled organisms and whether they can experience pain. The students could then explore questions about living and dying, or pain and suffering. Within such broad lessons, educators can introduce students to the "grays" of concepts—helping them see that ideas are not simply right or wrong

(Afflerbach & VanSledright, 2001). This can help students understand that answers to questions such as what it means to be alive can have multiple interpretations that are defensible.

Thus, our suggestion is that educators facilitate discussions about fundamental, ontological elements so that students can explore what they know and believe. Discussions of prior knowledge can also promote accretion and fine tuning (Rumelhart & Norman, 1981). In other words, administrators can help teachers choose and implement educational programs that enable students to enrich their conceptual knowledge by exposing them to rich and inviting experiences. From these experiences, students can develop more sophisticated conceptions.

Plausible New Theories

When introducing potentially conflicting ideas, educators must remember that their students may well hold alternative viewpoints that they are not willing to abandon easily. There are several factors that teachers should consider when attempting to replace students' naïve or inaccurate theories with more viable alternatives (Chinn & Brewer, 1993). Teachers must take care to make sure that the alternative theory is *intelligible, plausible*, and *compelling*.

First, educators must ask whether the theory they are offering will be comprehensible and intelligible to their students. Students are unlikely to accept a new theory they cannot understand. The theory must also be presented in language that is age-appropriate. Second, students should have ample opportunities to apply the new information in realistic situations. If they cannot apply the new theory, they are unlikely to accept it. The alternative theory should seem plausible or reasonable to the students based on their life experiences. Finally, in order for the new theory to be convincing or compelling, it needs to be sufficiently detailed and illustrated. Simply mentioning a theory and assuming it will be understood and accepted is pedagogically unwise.

Use of Anomalous Data

Research also suggests that, at times, students lack data, evidence, and arguments that are convincing enough to spark reconceptualization. Under these circumstances, if teachers want evidence to penetrate and contribute to a new conceptualization, they must support their explanations with data that students would find credible and unambiguous. In addition, teachers need to support their contentions in multiple ways with evidence from multiple sources (Murphy, 1998).

Murphy (2001) found that college students and experts were more convinced when they were provided with multiple forms of evidence (e.g., charts, graphs, strong arguments, or personal vignettes). These findings suggest that change is more likely in young minds if learning is multisensory; that is, if students, especially young students, hear, see, and physically engage an idea (Piaget, 1952). Moreover, regardless of age, students are more likely to experience conceptual change when anomalous data are confronted on multiple, seemingly independent occasions. Otherwise, students' emerging concepts remain fragile and easily disassembled by more intuitively comfortable interpretations (Hynd, Alvermann, & Qian, 1997).

Encouraging Deeper Processing

Finally, there is ample evidence to suggest that conceptual change requires deep-level versus superficial processing (e.g., Petty & Cacioppo, 1986). That is to say, simply passing one's mind over new, conflicting ideas or quickly trying them on for size does not ensure that those ideas will be well perceived or ultimately adopted.

To complete this type of deep processing, students will require strategies (Chapter 5). Strategies help students to probe and question, to reflect and summarize (Garner, 1990). Strategies allow students to consider evidence and weigh its credibility (Alexander et al., 1998). Strategies also have the potential to help students synthesize information from multiple sources in order to form a tentative theory or explanation (Pressley, Goodchild, Fleet, Zajchowski, & Evans, 1989). Such intertextual and intratextual processing is particularly important in the new multimedia environments. The more such mental tools students have available, the greater their chances of achieving conceptual change and development (Perkins & Simmons, 1988).

Materials for Promoting Change

A variety of classroom materials have been used to foster conceptual change. One of the most powerful tools for this purpose is refutational text. In particular, the social and educational psychology literatures have shown that two-sided refutational texts are particularly effective at changing students' misconceptions (Allen et al., 1994; Guzzetti & Hynd, 1998). *Two-sided refutational texts* are constructed so that both sides of an issue are presented, and then one side of the plausible argument is refuted or dismantled (Murphy, 1998). Unfortunately, most textbooks are one-sided in nature. For example, an elementary textbook on animal classification would simply describe the way scientists sort and classify animals and discuss the benefits of sorting animals this way. In contrast, a two-sided refutational textbook would likely introduce how nonscientists (i.e., young children) sort and categorize animals. Then, the author would go on to argue for an alternative classification scheme (i.e., the scheme used by experts), while systematically pointing out the weaknesses or flaws of less scientific schemes.

What appears to make two-sided refutational texts so successful at sparking change is that they promote a number of the mechanisms outlined by Chinn and Brewer (1993). That is, effective two-sided refutational texts bring common misconceptions to the surface, make compelling arguments, and offer useful examples and illustrations in meaningful contexts.

How Do Instructional Leaders Put Knowledge Research Into Practice?

There are many actions that administrators and teachers can take to orchestrate learning environments that encourage students to assume their roles as active, reflective thinkers who weigh the arguments they read or hear, probe for additional information, consider alternative explanations, and weigh the source of any seemingly relevant information. Specifically, we offer several possible guiding principles for administrators and teachers to use in helping students acquire and alter relevant academic knowledge.

- **Students' understandings, beliefs, and interests, rather than those of the teacher or curriculum supervisor, must be the central starting point for meaningful instruction**

Educators frame the instructional experiences around what they deem important, hopefully based on a principled understanding of the domain of study. Too often, however, administrators and teachers assume either that their students have no prior knowledge in the area or that their naïve understandings do not play a role in instruction. Educational professionals cannot become complacent in their instructional design and assume that they have a clear picture of students' existing base of knowledge, their relevant beliefs, or their interests (Dienes & Berry, 1997). It is wise, especially for teachers, to take some time to unearth critical information before introducing new and potentially conflicting information. As the instructional leaders in schools, administrators should provide teachers with opportunities to investigate different curricular programs and learn about different teaching methods. Moreover, having uncovered such information, educators should acknowledge students' understandings and infuse those perspectives into instruction in positive and nonjudgmental ways.

- **Administrators and teachers must ensure that high-quality oral discussions and written texts are used in schools and classrooms**

What is evident in the change literature is that the messages that students read or hear *do* have a direct effect on what they come to understand (Chambliss, 1995; Murphy & Alexander, 2004). For this reason, administrators and teachers should play a joint role in the selection of well-crafted textbooks and in incorporating those textbooks in classrooms where oral discussions are commonplace. Texts, whether delivered orally or in writing, serve to frame the discussion in terms of arguments and evidence and as a resource for alternative theories and multiple perspectives on issues or concepts (Chambliss & Garner, 1996; Hynd, Alvermann, & Qian, 1997). Of course, book selection is sometimes out of the control of administrators and teachers. When this is the case, teachers must be given the resources necessary to supplement and extend existing texts when the need arises.

For example, because curriculum development in her state is primarily under the auspices of the state superintendent's office, Mrs. Bridges was concerned that the 7th graders in her social studies classes would not be adequately exposed to the rich Navajo heritage within the local community. When she approached the principal, Mrs. Driskill, about this issue, Mrs. Driskill assured Mrs. Bridges that she would be happy to see the local Navajo history infused into the school's 7th-grade social studies curriculum. With Mrs. Driskill's support and encouragement, Mrs. Bridges also used some of the instructional fund to take her students on a field trip to an ancient Navajo site in the next county.

- **Administrators and teachers should present themselves as but one credible source of information in the school and classroom**

Educators are probably aware that students play a kind of game in which they attempt to figure out answers their teachers are looking for with as little effort as possible. In such a situation, meaningful learning is hard to achieve, and the teacher serves as the sole source of information. Likewise, some teachers may mistakenly assume that their job is simply to do as they are told by school administrators rather than to engage in deep processing or reflection about the content or pedagogical techniques (Petty & Cacioppo, 1986). Clearly, students are unlikely to manifest critical and reflective thinking if they risk ridicule or reprimand any time they pose alternative explanations or counterarguments. Teachers and administrators must foster open and risk-free environments, both in their classrooms and in faculty or departmental meetings, in which they remove themselves from the role of the one true authority if deep processing and conceptual change are to be promoted.

However, we are not suggesting that administrators and teachers should avoid evaluative comments or shy away from presenting prevailing views. We do not think complete relativity is the answer. Rather, educators need to see themselves as credible and reliable sources of information—just not the sole source. Educators should allow some activities in the classroom to be student-led or student-directed so that the role of authority is shifted and students have the opportunity for greater self-determination (Ryan & Deci, 2000). For example, teachers could allow students to select among possible activities or experiences for their unit on animal classifications. Should they watch the video about animals, read a book about animal classifications, or look up some information on the computer? Likewise, administrators should also allow the teachers they supervise to have input in the content of school meetings and into the policies and procedures formulated to deal with instructional and personnel problems that arise.

- **Teach students how to frame sound arguments and provide support for their assertions**

Often, students have relevant ideas that could be shared in the course of instruction, but they elect to remain silent. The reasons for this situation are varied, but the literature suggests that people are more likely to offer an alternative viewpoint if they feel they have the communication and social skills to do so adequately (Anderson, Chinn, Chang, Waggoner, & Yi, 1997). Yet the skills of argumentation and persuasion do not come naturally or easily (Toulmin, 1958).

Individuals ill-equipped with skills of argument often support their contentions with non-evidence-based statements—statements that might begin with "I believe so" or "because it's so." Such statements do not serve as adequate substantiation, and they are unlikely to convince anyone. If we are to advance the change process, we must be able to offer convincing evidence or compelling examples to support positions (Toulmin, 1958). This is hard for many adults and most students. However, research shows that students as young as nine or ten can be taught how to recognize weak and strong arguments in text and to develop sound arguments of their own (Chambliss & Murphy, 2002; VanSledright, 1996).

Administrators and teachers need to function as models of reflection, analysis, and argumentation. As we will discuss in Chapter 6, educators can ask many types of questions. Nystrand (2003) refers to questions for which the educators do not have ready-made answers as "authentic" questions. When educators ask more complex and thought-provoking questions, they soon find that the process of formulating a reasonable response is certainly as important to evaluate in their students as whether those students get a "right" answer. Indeed, when knowledge acquisition and alternation are the goal, it is particularly important for educators to evaluate the alternative perspectives that students introduce (Campione, Shapiro, & Brown, 1995; Garner, 1990). In effect, in thought-provoking learning environments, the *processes* of reasoning and problem solving are as critical as the *product* of those efforts.

Another reason to begin evaluating the process as well as the product is that students will often do what is required to get a good grade in class. Moreover, they will do so even if that means suppressing their own beliefs or understandings in favor of the position espoused by the classroom authority, particularly their teacher or their textbook (Alexander, Jetton, Kulikowich, & Woehler, 1994). When Alexander and colleagues interviewed students in science classes, some of the brightest commented that they occasionally gave answers that they knew were wrong, but they knew these were the answers their teachers expected. As we will discuss in Chapter 4, it is often as important—if not more so—to students to respond correctly to please the teacher or administrator than it is to seek the most plausible or viable conclusion.

Chapter Reflections

As we learned in this chapter, the acquisition and alteration of knowledge can be a challenging task, particularly when those ideas are long held and deeply rooted. However, the insights gained from the literatures in knowledge acquisition and knowledge and beliefs can be invaluable resources for educators who want to stimulate profound and enduring change in their students. In this chapter we discussed three states of knowledge (i.e., declarative, procedural, and conditional), and we highlighted the importance of each in the learning process.

We also discussed the processes of acquiring and changing knowledge. Across the processes of acquiring and altering knowledge, we offered several guiding points. First, students' knowledge is as unique as their fingerprints. For that reason, teachers must expect differences in students' construction, interpretation, and communication of their understandings. In addition, teachers must become masters at recognizing the patterns in students' thinking and at appreciating that their shared understandings are probably based on a system of logic that may not be interpretable at first.

In addition, existing knowledge is the key to future knowledge. Decades of research have led to the realization that existing knowledge dramatically shapes what students come to learn. Thus, teachers must routinely seek to uncover what their students know or believe, and this prior knowledge must serve as the foundation for future learning. Likewise, administrators and teachers need to look thoughtfully at the curriculum and activities they incorporate in schools and classrooms in order to determine what those tasks require.

Finally, the person, materials, and the context influence the process of learning. Indeed, knowledge is never context-free (see Table 3.4). Therefore, effective educators must work to create rich and stimulating learning environments that support knowledge construction. Moreover, educators would be wise to formulate extensive and meaningful experiences to which instructional tasks and social interactions can be appropriately anchored. Classroom discussions can be used as a window into students' understanding before and after the learning experience.

Table 3.4   Linking Principles of Knowledge With Effective Instructional
                  Practice

Knowledge Principles	Putting Principles Into Practice
Students' knowledge is as unique as their fingerprints.	Administrators and teachers should: • Expect diversity in students' responses and interpretations. • Be attentive to the patterns in students' knowledge, whether those patterns are typical or atypical.
Students' existing knowledge is a powerful determiner of what they will learn in the future.	Administrators and teachers should: • Take time to activate relevant background knowledge. • Consider what each task or activity will require of students.
Students' knowledge is also shaped by time and place.	Administrators and teachers should: • Ensure that learning environments are resource-rich. • Anchor new or challenging experiences to those that are more familiar and well-practiced.
Students' knowledge guides their views of and interactions with the world.	Administrators and teachers should: • Link the activities within schools and classrooms to the world outside. • Let students' everyday lives serve as a scaffold for their educational experiences.
Students' knowledge is always social and cultural in nature.	Administrators and teachers should: • Ensure that the experiences of nonmajority cultures are valued aspects in the educational experience. • Be models of knowledge-seeking for their students.

4

Cultivating
Student Motivation

Guiding Questions

- What does it mean to be motivated?
- How do students' goals and competency beliefs relate to their learning and achievement?
- What can instructional leaders do to foster motivation in students?

What Does It Mean to Be Motivated?

According to national surveys and educational research, lack of academic interest, involvement, or engagement is pervasive (Rock, Owings, & Lee, 1994). Whatever excitement or passion for learning young children bring into the classroom in their early years begins to fade with each passing year of schooling (Wigfield et al., 1996). A significant decline in students' interest in educational pursuits emerges in early adolescence and persists throughout public schooling (Wigfield, 1993). Middle-school students surveyed as part of the National Assessment of Educational Progress (Carnegie Council on Adolescent Development, 1996) became increasingly less involved in academic activities between the 4th and 8th grades. Because of this decline, motivation is one of the most serious concerns of practicing teachers.

Administrators and teachers must cope with this lack of interest and involvement among students, and with students' competing needs and goals, both inside and outside the classroom. Students have a right to sense the beauty and power that deep knowledge and understanding can afford. Educational leaders and educators must discover ways to catch and keep student interest and to maintain student engagement in educational experiences they find personally rewarding, meaningful, and intellectually enriching (Alexander & Murphy, 1993). The first step in transforming learning into such a positively motivating experience for all members of the classroom community is to come to grips with the nature of motivation. Until they understand what motivation entails, administrators and teachers have little hope of orchestrating an educational experience that fosters optimal engagement and fulfillment (Pintrich & Schunk, 2001).

Motivations (see Table 4.1) are the psychological processes "involved in the direction, vigor, and persistence of behavior" (Bergin, Ford, & Hess, 1993, p. 437). Motivation is the fuel that propels us forward toward a desired goal or end. Individuals who are highly motivated face academic problems with a well-honed sense of energy and personal commitment (Pintrich & Schunk, 2001). By comparison, less motivated students wander aimlessly or with only a vague end in mind. Although some students may seem unmotivated, positive motivations underlie every successful human action, whether that action is practicing an instrument every day, working on school assignments, or writing this chapter. Thus, it is probably fair to say

Table 4.1   Definitions of Relevant Terms

Term	Definition	Example
Achievement Motivation	Goal-directed actions aimed at bringing about success in school.	*Most of the instructional leadership decisions administrators make are powered by their goal that all students achieve academically.*
Attributions	Causal statements about the conditions or circumstances that underlie successes or failures.	*Teachers hear many explanations from students about why they performed poorly on a particular exam. Those explanations can range from bad luck (i.e., external, uncontrollable) to lack of concentration (internal, controllable).*

Term	Definition	Example
Controllability	Whether individuals attribute their success or failure to factors they see as within their control.	*When a principal's school reports a decline in the state reading assessment, she decides that there are critical steps she can institute to bring about improvement.*
Fundamental Attribution Error	Misjudgments leading students to attribute their performance erroneously to a source.	*When students fail to prepare for an exam, they sometimes attribute their failure to the test maker or the teacher. This would be a fundamental attribution error pertaining to locus.*
Goal	Target or end point to which individuals aspire academically or socially.	*School administrators in Xavier district adopt the goal of raising their achievement scores by 5 percent over last year's scores.*
Goal Orientations	Set of behavioral intentions that determine how individuals approach and engage in learning activities.	*Students' goals orientations can vary from wanting to learn for the sake of learning or learning to get grades to just get through the work with the least amount of effort.*
Learned Helplessness	Belief that nothing you do can help you learn, associated with negative attributions that are internal and uncontrollable.	*Mr. Skylar had a student who believed that she was terrible at mathematics and who failed at every task.*
Learning Goals Synonyms: Mastery Goals, Task Goals	Represents a desire to develop competence, increased knowledge or understanding through effortful learning.	*Jeff and Margery are two students in Ms. Graves's Advanced English class who are more concerned with understanding the content than in impressing her with their knowledge.*
Locus	Where students place credit or blame for their performance.	*Teachers sometimes blame their students' performance on the influence of standardized achievement tests, a condition outside their influence.*

(Continued)

Table 4.1 (Continued)

Term	Definition	Example
Motivation	Psychological process involved in the direction, vigor, and persistence of behavior.	*Administrators are often highly motivated to support their teachers in their professional development pursuits.*
Performance Goals	Represents a desire to gain favorable judgments and avoid negative judgments of one's competence.	*The students in Mr. Simmons's classes who were merely trying to impress him with their questions were exhibiting performance goals.*
Self-Efficacy Beliefs	People's judgments about their capabilities to organize and execute courses of action required to attain designated types of performances.	*Because of her years as a debate team member, Miss Percy felt confident that she could present her case for a new curriculum innovation effectively to the school board.*
Social Goals	Goals whose ends pertain to social relationships or to performing in ways that are socially acceptable.	*Elementary-school principals and teachers are often very concerned about students' prosocial behaviors. They want students to learn how to behave in appropriate ways in the classroom.*
Work-Avoidant Goals	Goals whose end is to exert the minimum effort on an academic task.	*The students in Mrs. Lawrence's class who did only enough work to get by were exhibiting work-avoidant goals.*

that all individuals are highly motivated at certain times and for certain things. The issue for teachers and administrators is how to direct students' inner energies toward things *academic*.

Educators at all levels need to know how to tap into the desires, wants, and passions of students and channel them toward the pursuit of academic understanding. How do we build a deep connection to learning in those whom we teach, so knowledge seeking is propelled from within rather than coerced or forced from without? Before we consider how to create learning environments that promote direction, energy, and commitment among students for academic goals, we examine the role that students' goals and their beliefs in their ability to succeed play in learning and achievement.

How Do Students' Goals and Competency Beliefs Relate to Their Learning and Achievement?

One characteristic that differentiates motivation from other constructs we have discussed is that motivation is necessarily goal-directed. In fact, some consider all motivation to be goal-directed behavior (Ford, 1992; Wentzel, 1991). Broadly defined, a goal is a target to which we aspire (Pintrich & Schunk, 2001), and goals are natural parts of our everyday existence. Some of the goals we establish for ourselves pertain specifically to learning or to school achievement (i.e., academic goals; Ford, 1992). The term *achievement motivation* signifies those goal-directed actions aimed at bringing about success in school (Murphy & Alexander, 2000).

At times, the academic goals students establish take on a pattern that is rather consistent across a range of academic tasks or learning situations. When this occurs, learners are said to have *goal orientations* (Ames, 1984; Miller, Greene, Montalvo, Ravindran, & Nichols, 1996). Meece, Blumenfeld, and Hoyle (1988) consider goal orientations to be a "set of behavioral intentions that determine how students approach and engage in learning activities" (p. 514). The orientations that students manifest relate significantly to their academic achievement.

Academic Goals

The different goal orientations students have toward learning translate into different learning outcomes, which is why the topic of goal orientations is important motivational territory for school administrators and teachers. Goal theories explain this interplay by positioning learners' goals in a comprehensive framework that encompasses such related factors as students' self-beliefs, their expectations, and their academic behaviors (Pintrich & Schunk, 2001).

Mastery and Performance Goals

In the goal theory literature, two contrasting perspectives toward academic engagement have been researched extensively (Ames & Archer, 1988): mastery and performance goals. *Learning* or *mastery goals* (Dweck & Leggett, 1988) represent increased knowledge and academic competence. Those with mastery goals want to understand what they are learning and pursue knowledge for its own sake. For example, students holding to mastery goals apply internal criteria for judging success, willingly work toward understanding, value what they learn, and take risks to achieve their ends.

On the other hand, *performance goals* (Dweck & Leggett, 1988) signify the learners' desire to do well on tasks, so as to receive recognition and outpace others or to avoid shame or embarrassment. Students with performance goals see success as competition and academic ranking. They tend to be cautious, so as to avoid errors or potential loss of status, and value grades over knowledge.

Work-Avoidant Goals

Motivation researchers, like practicing teachers, are well aware that certain students have little interest in educational pursuits, whether for self-enrichment or academic competition. Another category of goal orientation, *work-avoidant goals* (Meece et al., 1988), has been added to capture this level of academic disengagement. The main concern of work-avoidant students is to finish work with a minimum of mental or physical effort (Meece & Holt, 1993). These students exhibit a minimalist orientation to schoolwork and learning and subsequently do not perform well on measures of academic achievement.

Many explanations can be forwarded for why students develop such negative attitudes toward academic work. For example, some work-avoidant students may simply see no value or purpose to their schoolwork, either for the short term (e.g., grades) or the long term (e.g., future success; Bandura & Schunk, 1981). Other students may complete only the problems they can finish in class on their mathematics homework because they believe that the assignment lacks value (Wigfield & Eccles, 1992). In other cases, work-avoidant students may find their schoolwork monotonous or unchallenging, as those studying gifted underachievers have reported (Stipek & Gralinski, 1996). Many classroom activities work to increase students' work-avoidant orientations by consistently underestimating students' ability or failing to provide them with sufficient challenge for extended periods of time (Miller, Behrens, Greene, & Newman, 1993).

Since not all students enjoy competition or social comparisons, a competitive classroom atmosphere may create social tensions for some students (Ames, 1992; Nichols, 1996). Those who thrive on competition may be in a better position than students who find peer comparisons disconcerting. Because work-avoidant students may feel socially ill at ease in the classroom, they may choose to withdraw from social competition or comparisons (Nicholls & Miller, 1994).

Another potential contributor to work-avoidant goals can be traced to students' beliefs about intelligence (Dweck, 1986; Stipek & Gralinski, 1996). Specifically, many students equate intelligence with the ability to succeed with limited effort (Alexander, 1985). Students who believe this may feel that any manifestation of effort is evidence of limited intellectual capacity and might risk poor grades rather than call their mental abilities into question. Work-avoidant students may also hold fatalistic attitudes about their performance. In other words, they may believe that their efforts will not have any real effect on their academic success or failure and thus will quit trying when they feel they are not gaining from their efforts.

Finally, we must consider that work-avoidant students have other needs that seem far more important or pressing and push schoolwork to the background (Ford, 1992; Wentzel, 1989). Students who are facing difficult situations in their family lives or are struggling with serious issues of self-esteem may have only limited energy to devote to an academic agenda.

Social Goals

Not all the goals that learners internalize are exclusively about academic performance. Some pertain to social relationships in the learning environment or to performing in ways that are socially acceptable or socially sanctioned. These forms of human pursuits are called *social goals* (Wentzel, 1991, 1999).

Social forces are much more influential to students' goals than most motivational researchers acknowledge (Wentzel, 2000). Even the questions used to establish goal orientations illustrate the strong undercurrent of social forces on students' learning and achievement. In other words, when students respond that they do their schoolwork so they do not look stupid or so they win the approval of classmates, they are showing evidence of social forces. Even those who set out to perform well so they compare favorably with their peers are responding to social factors.

Social factors are undeniable forces in academic performance, as evidenced in earlier research of human needs, drives, and academic goals. For example, the belonging need described in Maslow's Hierarchy (1954) relates to students' social goals. This need is often exhibited in students' efforts to understand and comply with the social codes of conduct in the classroom (Wentzel, 2000). Thus, students generally sit politely at their desks or tables, enter discussions at appropriate times, and recognize the social hierarchy present.

The belonging need also manifests itself in the relationships and friendships students form in the learning environment (Youniss & Smollar, 1989). Such social relationships can vary in their importance from student to student and from year to year. In other words, some students have strong needs to be popular, socially connected to a large number of others. Other students are content with having one or two close friends.

Of course, during middle school and high school, the influence of peers increases in importance (Eccles & Midgley, 1990). What class-mates think, for better or worse, colors students' views of learning and achievement. Approximately one quarter of 4th and 8th graders admit that their friends make fun of students who try hard in school (Wentzel, 1999). Such negative perceptions of academic effort among friends may dampen students' willingness to display enthusiasm for their schoolwork.

Social beliefs and ensuing goals can sometimes complement students' academic goals, making learning and achievement more likely (Wentzel, 1996). For example, if students believe that the most popular students are also the smartest students in their class, they may devote more energy to their studies to attempt to increase their own popularity. Similarly, if students enjoy working collaboratively with others, their own understanding and performance might be enhanced. On the other hand, social and academic goals can be at odds, resulting in limited engagement. For instance, students who see school as principally a place to make friends may be less likely to dedicate their energies to academic tasks. This is especially true when they or their friends hold negative perceptions of hardworking or enthusiastic students.

Competency Beliefs

The determinations they make as to why good or bad things happen to them and the judgments that students form about their abilities have a great deal of influence on their achievement. This realization became the basis for programs of research in attributions and efficacy judgments (e.g., Graham & Weiner, 1996). Simply stated, whenever students face surprising or significant outcomes they can-not help but react emotionally and cognitively (Weiner, 1991). How they react not only signals their motivational state but also hints at their academic self-concept and their likelihood of later achieve-ment. For example, to what do students attribute their apparent suc-cess or failure in a given situation? Is a student's actual performance commensurate with anticipated performance? Do students believe that performance now or in the future is within their control, or are they just hapless academic victims?

Attributions: Who's to Blame?

The rationalizations and justifications that students make are called *attributions* (Weiner, 1986). Attributions are causal statements about the conditions that underlie apparent successes or failures. When events occur, whether positive or negative, we try to fit those events into our existing beliefs about ourselves and the world. In other words, students attempt to make sense of academic events by taking credit or placing blame in accordance with their preconceptions of themselves as learners. The place of this division forms the foundation of students' causal attributions (Weiner, 1972). From extensive research on students' attributions, Bernard Weiner (1991) developed a theory explaining the nature of these causal judgments. Weiner identified several components to students' attributions. Of primary importance for this discussion are two of those concepts: locus and controllability (see Table 4.2).

Table 4.2　　Two Dimensions of Attributions: Locus and Control

		LOCUS	
		INTERNAL	EXTERNAL
CONTROLLABILITY	UNCONTROLLABLE	APTITUDE MOOD/ILLNESS	LUCK TASK/DOMAIN CHARACTERISTICS
	CONTROLLABLE	EFFORT PERSISTENCE	INSTRUCTIONAL CONDITIONS TEACHER/PEER ASSISTANCE

Locus. One of the most potent characteristics of causal judgments, *locus*, deals with where students place credit or blame. In particular, students either see the cause as within them (i.e., *internal locus*) or they attribute cause to external forces (i.e., *external locus*). For example, in thinking that strong performance on a test results from their talent in science, students are associating their performance with an internal condition, ability in science. In contrast, if students credit their poor performance to the poor instruction they received, they are making an external attribution.

Individuals who tend toward internal over external judgments typically feel that their behaviors are meaningfully linked to resulting outcomes (Graham & Weiner, 1996). Therefore, these internally oriented students see their rewards and punishments as reflections of their efforts, skills, or abilities. Those who tend to focus on external causes are more apt to see the outcomes of actions as more the effect of chance or random occurrence. For this reason, externally oriented students are more apt to call upon fate, luck, or other people when rationalizing their performance (Weiner, 1986).

Controllability. When researchers first talked about the locus dimension, they used the phrase "locus of control." But Weiner (1972) held that this concept actually has two separate dimensions: locus *and* control. *Controllability* refers to whether students see the factors associated with their success or failure as within their personal control (i.e., *controllable*) or whether they think these factors lie outside their direct control (i.e., *uncontrollable*). If a student, Michael, believes that he could have done better on his theater arts audition if he had spent more time learning his lines, he would be forwarding a controllable explanation. In contrast, if the student, Rose, felt that her performance during the audition was not great, but was the best she could have done, she would be identifying a causal condition that she cannot personally control. The locus remains internal, but controllability of the action differs from the prior case.

Motivational researchers still debate the controllable/external issue (Stipek, 1988). Can some factor be external to the individual and still be perceived as controllable? According to Weiner, some situations can be both controllable and external (Weiner, 1991). For example, if a teacher scored an essay low because she was biased against the student, the circumstance would be external to the student. However, it is still within the teacher's control to eliminate the bias. Stipek (1988) and others disagree with this analysis and argue that *any* external cause must be judged uncontrollable by default. A position between these two extremes can be taken. First, the value of attribution theory lies in understanding how students perceive the circumstances of their successes or failures. That pertains to the dimension of control. That is, for circumstances to be judged controllable, students must see the situation as in their control and not the domain of others, like administrators, teachers, parents, or peers.

Building on an extensive literature, Pintrich and Schunk (2001) identified some common misjudgments that lead students to make erroneous and potentially harmful attributions. Pintrich and Schunk call these undesirable situations common attributional biases. Students sometimes overlook conditions within the immediate situation and attribute outcomes to traitlike factors, such as physical appearance or sociocultural factors. Jumping to conclusions based on appearance or other external features of those involved is a common case of a *fundamental attribution error*. Or a student might let his negative opinion of a previous teacher influence his interpretations of his current teacher.

Efficacy Judgments

Students also hold beliefs about their own abilities to succeed at specific tasks or in specific domains, formed in the past by their attributions of success or failure. These self-judgments are called *self-efficacy beliefs* (Bandura, 1977). Although linked to attributions, self-efficacy beliefs are unique in several ways. For one, self-efficacy beliefs are future-oriented (Bandura, 1982), representing beliefs about future success rather than analyses of past successes or failures. Also, these judgments about domain-specific or task-specific competencies arise from multiple sources other than causal attributions. Specifically, Bandura and Schunk (1981) hold that self-efficacy beliefs come from:

- *Past successes or failures within the domain or with similar tasks.* When confronted with a similar situation, did the student experience success or difficulty?
- *Comments from others, including teachers, peers, or parents.* What do others say to students about their capabilities or incompetencies?
- *Vicarious reactions to others within their academic, social, or cultural circles.* What do students see happening to others with whom

they relate, or what do they hear said to those with whom they identify?

- *Physiological states.* Do students' hearts race or their palms sweat when they are presented with certain tasks?

Consequences of Competency Judgments

These competency judgments can come with serious performance consequences. For example, what if you believed strongly that nothing you did as a student could help you to learn—that your fate as a low-performing student was sealed? How would you feel and behave? A belief in this seemingly endless cycle of failure and negative emotions or attributions is called *learned helplessness* (Peterson, Maier, & Seligman, 1993). As distressing as it may seem, a small percentage of students carry around such negative beliefs about themselves and their place in the learning community (Maier & Seligman, 1976). How this cycle begins is not clear, but students with learned helplessness come to perceive each failure as undeniable evidence that their mental aptitudes are low (Seligman, 1975). Even when they succeed, these students attribute their success to luck or an easy task rather than to effort or skill. Over time, these students simply come to expect failure, and thus respond to challenges with apathy or resignation.

The contrast between these learned-helpless students and highly successful, learning-oriented students can be quite dramatic (Schunk, 2000). These consequences extend to almost every dimension of learning, from perceptions of intelligence and beliefs in effort to valuing of knowledge and challenge. Learned-helpless students see intelligence as fixed and unchanging, effort as ineffective, and knowledge as personally meaningless, whereas learning-oriented students feel that they can improve through hard work and by learning more (Seligman, 1975).

Moreover, learned-helpless students do not expect much of themselves and easily give up when difficulties arise (Hardre & Reeve, 2003), whereas learning-oriented students maintain high expectations of themselves and are persistent even in the face of significant difficulty (Reeve, 1996). Learned-helpless students do not always know how to help themselves academically. Because their repertoire of strategies is limited and ineffective, learned-helpless students avoid potentially challenging situations and experience pervasive failure and high anxiety when they cannot avoid them. Learning-oriented students, on the other hand, are well equipped strategically to deal with problem situations and are confident in their own abilities. Thus, they seek out challenge and infrequently face failure or experience high anxiety.

What Can Instructional Leaders Do to Foster Motivation in Students?

The power of students' needs, drives, and goals to foster their learning and academic achievement is undeniable. Yet, the ability of students to translate these factors into optimal learning depends on the nature of the learning environment (Blumenfeld, 1992; Butler, 1994). From an attributional standpoint, administrators and teachers can control some aspects of the learning environment that either operate as a barrier to optimal learning or bolster the positive motivations students bring to the classroom. We offer several guidelines for fostering student motivation.

- **Make motivation a primary focus in the learning environment**

Educators must be proactive and explicitly work to create learning environments that spark motivation. Positive motivation does not just happen, even for teachers who are concerned about students' engagement in the learning environment (Brophy, 1998; Stipek, 1993). One important step in this process is being sensitive to students' signals about their motivation level. Not all students are clear about their motivational state. In fact, many younger students lack the ability or security to be outspoken and direct with school administrators or teachers about their needs and goals. Also, students may not interpret their feelings and actions in the way an experienced, sensitive adult can. For this reason, administrators and teachers need to be on the lookout for even subtle indicators of emerging motivational problems (Maehr, 1982).

For instance, Mr. Koestner, a dedicated new teacher at Forrester Elementary School, had problems maintaining his third graders' attention during reading and mathematics. When he spoke to Mr. Gernovich, his principal, about his concern, Mr. Gernovich assured him that this was a common problem with teachers—even veteran instructors. Building on Mr. Koestner's individual problem, Mr. Gernovich decided to devote one of the professional development days to the subject of student motivation. He invited a professor from the local university to speak on the topic of "Learner Goals and Ways to Increase Students' Motivation to Learn."

Following this presentation, the teachers, including Mr. Koestner, met and developed specific strategies they would use in their classrooms to promote students' motivation to learn. They decided they would use interest inventories to identify students' favorite reading topics and out-of-school hobbies (e.g., sports, cars, and music) that might involve mathematics. Then, during the semester, each teacher would consciously build on students' favorite topics when selecting reading materials or constructing practice problems. In addition, the teachers would find ways to incorporate students' personal interests into mathematics assignments or special reading projects. After using these motivational strategies for a semester, Mr. Koestner reported a marked improvement in the students' attention during reading and mathematics instruction.

In Table 4.3, we offer some guiding questions that can signal the onset of motivational problems (Stipek, 1988). Educators and educational leaders should respond to these questions after observing students on multiple occasions and under varying academic contexts. Any "no" response to an item on this list might suggest a budding motivational difficulty and should receive a teacher's immediate attention.

- **Build on students' existing needs,
  drives, goals, and personal interests**

In order to promote optimal learning, administrators and teachers must learn to tap the internal energy students bring with them into the classroom (Hidi, 1990). The most potent motivational energies come from within the student in the form of unvoiced needs, drives, and goals (Ryan & Deci, 2000). They also exist as personal or individual interests, such as hobbies or avocations (Alexander & Murphy, 1993).

However, students are not typically forthcoming about their self-beliefs or their personal interests and values. It is even likely that students have not expressly considered these important dimensions in light of their learning or achievement (Pintrich, 2003). Thus, if teachers are to succeed in creating a positive and enriching learning environment that targets individual strengths and needs, they must become skilled at uncovering students' beliefs, perceptions, goals, and values (Alexander & Dochy, 1995).

If educators want more direct access to such information, they must ask questions or pose situations that speak to these internal beliefs and perceptions (Murphy, 1998). Inventories or surveys are

Table 4.3   Examining Students' Motivations

Gauging Motivation Through Questions

Does the student:

- Pay attention to the teacher?
- Volunteer answers in class?
- Begin work on tasks immediately?
- Maintain attention until tasks are completed?
- Persist in trying to solve problems rather than giving up as soon as a problem appears to be difficult to solve?
- Work autonomously whenever possible?
- Ask for assistance when it is really needed?
- Turn assignments in on time?
- Turn in complete work?
- Select challenging courses and tasks, even though he or she might not initially succeed?
- Accept initial errors or less-than-perfect performance as a natural part of learning a new skill?
- Perform in a fairly uniform way on different tasks that require similar skills?
- Perform in a manner that reflects as high a level of understanding as his or her assignments?
- Engage in learning activities beyond course requirements?
- Appear happy, proud, enthusiastic, and eager in learning situations?
- Follow directions?
- Strive to improve his or her skill, even when he or she performs well relative to peers?
- Initiate challenging learning activities on his or her own?
- Work hard on tasks when not being graded?

SOURCE: Adapted from Stipek, D. J. (1988). *Motivation to learn: From theory to practice.* Englewood Cliffs, NJ: Prentice-Hall. p. 14.

additional tools that administrators and teachers can use to uncover students' interests and hobbies. Matching curriculum to students' interests, both in and out of school, during planning and implementation can bolster students' motivation in a classroom. These measures can consist of just a few general questions, such as:

> Do you have any particular hobbies or special talents?
>
> What do you like to do when you have free time?
>
> What was the last book you read for pleasure?

More particular inventories can target specific subject matter areas. For instance, one series of reading and listening interest inventories targets students at different grade levels. That is not to say that self-reported data are flawless or unquestionable (Ericsson & Simon, 1980; Pressley & Afflerbach, 1995). We recognize that students may respond in ways they see as socially acceptable, even though it is not an honest reflection of their personal views. Still, well-phrased questions can prove useful, especially when there is a pattern to what students reveal. Administrators should encourage their teachers to effectively question students to explore their expectancy beliefs as well as their beliefs about gender or stereotypes (Wigfield & Eccles, 2000) in order to determine the influences on their causal attributions.

Bandura and Schunk (1981) have used other approaches that teachers can apply in the classroom to examine students' self-efficacy beliefs. Specifically, they have presented students with a particular task, such as a series of word problems, and asked the students how successful they think they would be at solving those problems. For example, a music teacher could present students with written excerpts of music and ask them how capable they feel they would be in playing the piece. The answers would allow the music teacher to gauge the amount of self-assurance students feel and the amount of support or scaffolding that may be needed.

However teachers go about it, they must secure meaningful and useful information about their students' self-belief systems (Alexander & Murphy, 1998a). Administrators should then help teachers make effective use of that information as they plan their curricula and evaluate their students' progress. Otherwise, they are more apt to fall back on vague and potentially misleading or stereotypical concepts—an action that will inhibit optimal learning and development.

• Challenge students' minds in meaningful ways

When students feel their time is wasted by demeaning or worthless tasks, educators may have to revert to educational bribery to keep them attentive and involved. However, as Ryan and Deci (2000) make clear, the long-term consequence of the "earn as you learn" approach exemplified by gold stars, bendy straws, or other trinkets is an erosion of the foundation of optimal learning. Dewey (1913) reminds us that education should not be portrayed as simply *ends* that must be reached, but as a *means* to higher states of human existence. Thus, for optimal learning to occur, students must engage in suitably challenging experiences. Their minds must be stretched by activities and discussions that require them to work hard to understand.

But challenge cannot be misperceived as just hard work. It must carry with it personal value (Csikszentmihalyi, 1990). Moreover, students must come to that task equipped with the knowledge and skills required to meet the challenge. Administrators should help teachers demand more of students by encouraging them to anchor learning and by remaining available to provide information and support if and when needed. Students will also accept academic challenges more readily when they feel they can take certain calculated risks and express their thoughts and wishes in the learning environment (Karabenick, 2004).

- ## Acknowledge students' efforts and accomplishments appropriately

Part of the risk taking just described rests on administrators' and teachers' responses to students' efforts and achievements in the classroom (Butler, 1994; Harter, 1996). It is very easy, given the nature of schooling, for educators to convey a belief that learning is a matter of social or normative comparison. Due to the manner in which grades are given or large-scale tests are conducted, students can see their own learning as hinging on the success or failure of others rather than on individual achievement.

However, for optimal learning to result, students must also feel that the school administration and their teachers are aware of their individual efforts and achievements, even when these accomplishments do not reach exceptional levels on a normative scale (Eccles, Midgley, & Adler, 1984). Administrators and teachers must ensure that students are judged on their personal progress toward established goals that are either spelled out in individual teacher-student contracts or related to independent projects and activities. Further, students should have opportunities to interact privately and personally with the school administration and their teachers about their personal needs and goals. Individual student conferences about classroom performance are one way to promote these types of personal interchanges in a private setting between administrators or teachers and the student. When educators listen to students in one-on-one settings, students feel as if their feelings, ideas, and interests are valued and may be more likely to exhibit more effort in the classroom.

Students must feel that their individual characteristics and abilities are recognized and appreciated (Eccles et al., 1998) through tasks assessed on jointly established criteria or not graded at all. Toward this end, administrators and teachers might consider making individual portfolios or individual progress charts a part of their systemic evaluation plans. This will also give educators a basis for guiding the learning and development of students, regardless of where those students presently stand on the road to self-fulfillment or self-actualization. In this way, students do not feel burdened with comparison and competition.

• Maintain high expectations for all students

Administrators and teachers must be sensitive to their own biases toward students perceived as less competent or less capable (Allington, 1980; Brophy, 1998). Educators cannot help but form broad ability judgments about their students. Teachers mentally sort students into more or less capable categories based on performance or other more insidious characteristics, including physical appearance, gender, ethnic stereotypes, or socioeconomic status.

Observational studies illustrate how educators unconsciously treat females and males differently in classrooms (Sadker & Sadker, 1994; Sadker, Sadker, & Klein, 1991). For example, teachers consistently report that girls participate more in their classrooms than boys. However, the videotapes of classroom instruction reveal quite a different story. In reality, the teachers tend to call on the males more than the females, give the boys more general, abstract questions to answer than girls and a longer time in which to respond, and are more apt to let males try again if they are unable to respond correctly at first.

This differential treatment has also been documented in educators' interactions with students thought to be low in academic ability (Allington, 1980). Teachers react differently to presumed low-ability students in their pattern of questions, in the assignments they make, and in the opportunities for choice and personal expression they provide (Ryan & Deci, 2000). Teachers might publicly acclaim that these students are able to learn, but their actual behaviors send a very different message to those students (Entwisle & Baker, 1983), a message likely to reinforce any negative self-beliefs that students harbor. These categorizations are present on an unconscious level, yet they influence the ways teachers treat their students in the classroom immensely (Brophy, 1999) and possibly the ways in which administrators deal with the concerns of teachers, students, and parents. Further, teachers must make certain that their curriculum includes material about the cultures of all students in their classes.

As the old adage goes, "actions speak louder than words." Therefore, administrators and teachers must be concerned that all students have sufficient time to think before responding and chances to rephrase or reevaluate their answers (Allington, 1980). All students must have a voice in classroom discussions and the occasion to explore tasks of personal value and interest (Alexander, 1997b). Moreover, all students need to feel that they are valued members of the classroom community who can work at times without direct supervision (Miserandino, 1996).

• Use feedback that highlights student effort and control

Like their behaviors, educators' verbal feedback to students can mold their attributions and self-competency beliefs (Brophy, 1998). As mentioned, teachers' evaluative comments can either promote feelings of control and increased effort or can exacerbate negative attributions (Graham, 1984; Weiner, Graham, Chandler, 1982). Effective feedback to students should regularly and systematically follow their actions and should address specific aspects of their performance (e.g., "Marcia, you have produced very rich colors in your self-portrait." Nafpaktitis, Mayer, & Butterworth, 1985). Further, feedback should refer directly to any agreed-upon performance criteria (e.g., "Marcia, you remember that we discussed having a sketch of your self-portrait project completed by October?" Brophy & Good, 1986).

Effective feedback does not mean avoiding critical comments. Students need to understand what they are doing well and what they need to improve (Bangert-Drowns, Kulik, Kulik, & Morgan, 1991; Elawar & Corno, 1985). Thus, evaluative comments cannot be routinely favorable, although they should be positively and sensitively framed. It must be noted, though, that even praise can be rightly or wrongly given (Ginott, 1972). Specifically, praise that is offered at the wrong time, as when work is mediocre or below the students' capabilities, or framed in the wrong way, can lead to negative attributions, lower expectations of success, or reduced valuing of academic tasks (Maier & Seligman, 1976).

If feedback is to enhance students' performance, it should offer clear information about the students' competence at specific tasks (Kohn, 1993). Educators should also compare students' current performance with what they have done the past (e.g., "Marcia, you are getting much better at creating perspective in your sketches.") as opposed to the work of other students (Brophy & Good, 1986). Moreover, administrators and teachers need to praise students' efforts, along with their abilities, particularly when the task is difficult and when some success is realized (e.g., "Your extra effort and your original idea for this self-portrait really came together in this creative work, Marcia." Natriello & Dornbusch, 1985). If students accept this type of constructive feedback from school administrators and their teachers, they may feel in greater control of their learning and be more willing to work hard in the future (Weiner, 1994).

Also, when educators make evaluative comments to students, they should talk in terms of the students' actions and skills and not in relation to their own actions or interpretations (Wlodkowski, 1985). The feedback is about the students and not the educator. Thus, rather than make a comment like "Marcia, *Mrs. Davis* gave you detention because . . ." administrators need to put the responsibility squarely on Marcia's shoulders (e.g., "Marcia, you earned detention in Mrs. Davis's room because . . .").

Finally, whatever the point being discussed or evaluated, administrators and teachers should be careful not to disrupt students' performance during processing, distracting them from their immediate goals (Brophy, 1998). Instead, attributional feedback should be rendered once that phase of the process is completed. This last recommendation is more easily accomplished when educators break a formidable task into components with an associated timeline. Administrators, teachers, and their students can discuss task performance at each of those designated points during the process without disrupting the students' thinking or learning.

- **Conceptualize motivation as a continuous, multifaceted, and developing process**

Finally, administrators and teachers must accept the varied and fluid nature of students' motivations. We are not the same individuals at 25 that we were at 5. Similarly, we must realize that motivation is not an all-or-nothing phenomenon. Motivation is a complicated, dynamic, and ongoing aspect of our lives (Bong, 1996; Wigfield et al., 1996). All the physical, emotional, social, and cognitive changes we experience throughout our lives alter our motivations. The significance of various motivations rises and falls, as does students' ability to take control over their needs and ensuing goals. This developmental perspective on motivation has significant implications for educators (Stipek, 1996).

First, it suggests that optimal learning is more likely to occur when educators focus early on students' needs, drives, and goals. It is never too early to concentrate on students' motivational well-being, but it can almost seem too late. Educators cannot wait until students are seniors in high school and then decide that they need to discover the positive character of learning. Young children's inquisitive nature and their desire to please others need to be cultivated and nurtured from day one.

Second, administrators and teachers must realize that students will not be equally motivated in all academic domains or with all school tasks (Pintrich & Schunk, 2001). Certain learning activities will be more stimulating and rewarding to students than others, and certain academic domains will be more relevant to students than others. Similarly, the reasons that students perform academic tasks will vary according to the perceived value and expectancies of particular tasks. This fluctuation is inevitable and not necessarily detrimental. Rather, using the strengths and interests of all students in the classroom can promote variety and excitement, thereby increasing student motivation. Administrators and teachers must be flexible enough to reevaluate the curriculum they jointly planned and reinforce students' efforts so that more positive strivings emerge whenever these fluctuations become significant.

Finally, academic motivations must be placed in a broad developmental context that acknowledges nonacademic needs, drives, and goals (Schunk, 2000; Wigfield et al., 1996). By understanding the progress and interplay of the cognitive, socioemotional, and physical developments discussed in Chapter 2, teachers can more effectively weigh the competing draws on students' motivational energies. For example, students in early adolescence are influenced by both the nature of their friendships and their beliefs about the school administrators' and their teachers' care of their socioemotional well-being. Not only do students' intense physical transformations make them more susceptible to declines in academic motivation, but also the rise in peer influences during this same period can either inhibit or spark academic goals. Academic motivations must always be considered as one piece of the complex interplay of all human strivings.

Chapter Reflections

The goals that students have for their participation in education have a very powerful effect on their learning and behaviors. Those who have investigated students' goals for academic achievement have uncovered three primary orientations. There are those who seek to learn or master the content presented to them and those who are more concerned with the accolades and recognition that come with academic success, or the shame or difficulties that accompany failure. Those manifesting learning goals and those exhibiting performance goals are joined by those who seek to avoid the work necessary for academic achievement.

Of course, there are other reasons for participation in the classroom community than academic achievement. For one, researchers have examined the social reasons for students' engagement or nonengagement in educational experiences. They have been able to identify types of social goals and the effects of such goals on students' subsequent growth and performance. Whether academic or social in nature, however, these goals are significant motivational forces that shape students' learning and development.

Humans cannot help but rationalize and justify their successes and failures. These rationalizations reveal their beliefs about their ability and help predict future justifications. Certain attributions have been tied to academic achievement, while others are indicative of learning problems. Such justifications provide clues to whether students attribute success or failure to forces within themselves (internal locus) or in the outside world (external locus). These statements also suggest whether students see these influential forces as stable, controllable, or uncontrollable.

However, students and teachers may make erroneous or harmful attributions. For example, when making a fundamental attribution error, students may credit their successes or failures to some basic disposition or personality trait. Whether accurate or inaccurate, competency beliefs come with consequences. For example, there are learned-helpless students who have entered into an endless cycle of failure and negative attributions. We have considered how these learned-helpless students compared to those with learning goal orientations and explored steps that administrators and teachers can take to help these students reframe their attributions.

If school administrators and teachers are proactive in fostering positive motivations among their students, then the serious declines and detachments witnessed among today's students can be channeled in more positive directions. At the very least, acting on the principles articulated in this chapter can serve as a starting point for promoting optimal learning for all students.

5

Strategic Learning and Strategic Teaching

Guiding Questions

- What does it mean to be a strategic learner?
- Are some basic strategies required to achieve academically?
- What principles can instructional leaders employ to promote students' strategic behavior?

What Does It Mean to Be a Strategic Learner?

At times we encounter problems, in and out of schools, that require us to think deeply and meaningfully about how to solve them. For instance, a young learner may come across a difficult passage in her 3rd-grade reader, and she finds that she does not understand it fully until she rereads it several times. Of course, difficulties in reading and understanding are not limited to young children. Recently, we were attempting to read directions for our rental car so that we could put the roof down. We found that the pictures were slightly more comprehensible than the poorly written text, so we relied solely on the pictures. Both of these situations required the use of strategies. The term *strategy* refers to mental operations or techniques used to solve problems or to enhance performance (Alexander & Jetton, 2000). Strategies come in multiple varieties (see Table 5.1 for a collection of relevant terms) and are more beneficial in some situations than they are in others. For example, some strategies help us understand and remember what we read or hear (Pressley et al., 1989), whereas others have more to do with keeping us focused and motivated in our learning (Winne, 1995). Similarly, some strategies are particularly useful at helping us capture and organize information (Armbruster, 2000). What should be evident is that strategic thinking can be useful in all aspects of lives.

At this point, it is important to differentiate strategies and strategic thinking from skills and skillful performance. Often the terms are used interchangeably, but they are quite different. Simply stated, when strategies have become routinized or habitualized, we refer to them as *skills*. As William James has suggested, skills are very much like mental habits (i.e., actions we typically take when faced with simple and highly familiar situations; James, 1890). Imagine the time it would take if you had to think deeply about how to open a door every time you encountered one. There is a high probability that we actually had to think about how to turn the doorknob at some point in our lives. Essentially, we perform skills at the subconscious level, and often they are so automatic that they require very little mental effort (Brown, 1975). It is important to note that skills are not innate abilities but techniques acquired and honed over time until they become automatic.

Are Some Basic Strategies Required to Achieve Academically?

Much of what we know about strategies resulted from research occurring in the 1980s (e.g., Anderson & Armbruster, 1984, 1986; Garner, 1987; Kierwa, 1989; Pressley, Levin, & Delaney, 1982; Weinstein & Mayer, 1986). At that time, an interesting debate took place regarding general and domain-specific strategies. Some researchers, like Robert Glaser (1984), argued that general strategies such as underlining or note taking are weak strategies. That means that these general strategies are tools that students use when they do not possess the particular knowledge that would produce a correct response or when they have no clear understanding of the problem at hand. To illustrate Glaser's position, let's consider two groups of graduate students, both of whom are taking an exam in an introductory statistics class.

Table 5.1   Definitions of Relevant Terms

Term	Definition	Example
Domain-Specific Strategies	Procedures typically applied in one or a few related fields.	*An algebra teacher instructs his students to use the FOIL method to make sure they use the appropriate combinations of terms when multiplying two binomials.*
General Strategies	Procedures that can be applied to a wide variety of tasks or domains.	*An elementary-school teacher reminds her students to use the techniques for summarization they have learned whenever needed, regardless of the subject.*
Intelligent Novices	Individuals capable of employing many general strategies skillfully, even when they confront novel tasks.	*Because Mr. Jenkins encouraged his high-school students to practice generalization, summarization, and asking questions with all types of content, his students are able to succeed when others falter.*
Metacognition	The process of reflecting upon and evaluating one's own thoughts and learning.	*During instruction on cell division, a biology teacher asks students to judge how well they understand the content and what they could do to learn more effectively.*
Skills	Procedures for thinking and behaving that have become routine.	*After years of practice, many of the students in Ms. Draco's 3rd-grade class are able to decode skillfully with minimal cognitive effort.*
Strategies	Mental operations or techniques used to solve problems or enhance performance.	*Administrators need to use a variety of strategies, including choosing words carefully and giving all relevant information in nonbiased ways, to calm disgruntled parents.*

The first group is armed with general strategies; they reflect on the problems, organize the information, seek help, and even motivate themselves to do well. The other group is armed with domain-specific, even problem-specific, strategies. This latter group of students will be far more successful at solving the problems efficiently and effectively than the group armed with only general strategies.

There is, however, another side to the coin. That is, as Robert Sternberg (1985) suggested, not all the problems students confront in schools have such clear and identifiable answers as introductory statistics problems. In addition, general strategies are useful to students in domains like math and science where the problems are well defined. For instance, the average statistics student still needs to be able to analyze problems, and middle-school science students still need to be able to outline their science texts. Further, reading comprehension seems to be at the heart of learning from texts, regardless of the domain of study (Graves, 1997). Certainly, reading comprehension plays a role in learning in almost every school subject.

We think that both sides are correct to a certain extent (Alexander & Murphy, 1998b). As Alexander (1997b) suggested, becoming competent in a field of study requires general strategies, as well as those that are more specific to a given domain. In science, for instance, high-school students need to know how to use a high-powered microscope and how to perform titration (i.e., the process of calculating the amount of a certain substance in a solution by systematically introducing another substance to that solution until a chemical change occurs). Likewise, 4th-grade students must learn the procedures for multiplying and dividing whole numbers.

The processes just described are all examples of *domain-specific strategies* because they are procedures typically applied in only one or a few related fields. Such procedures stand in contrast to *general strategies* (e.g., capturing and retaining information, and monitoring or regulating performance) that work for a broad range of tasks in many domains. It is conceivable that domain-specific strategies may be more prevalent in certain domains (e.g., mathematics or science; Spiro, Feltovich, Jacobson, & Coulson, 1992), whereas general strategies may be more pervasive in others (e.g., reading, writing, or history). In effect, for optimum achievement, students must possess both general strategies and domain-specific strategies.

Stocking a Strategy Toolbox

To perform a task like fixing a leaky faucet or even baking a cake adequately, you need the right tool. Strategies are very much like tools. Students need to be able to reach into their strategy toolboxes and select the correct tool to perform a given task (Paris et al., 1983;

Paris et al., 1991). You only have to tackle a few problems before you realize that you are far better off if you have an extensive set of tools from which to choose. Table 5.2 represents a range of general learning and studying strategies documented in the literature. The strategies in Table 5.2 are organized into six broad categories. As we discuss in this chapter, some strategies enable students to locate and construct somewhat permanent mental records of fleeting information. Having captured information, students need strategies to help them organize the information. Organized information is more likely to be retained in memory. At times, however, we also need strategies to augment and enhance our memories. Students must also possess strategies to self-motivate, especially when faced with extremely difficult tasks. The last category of strategies pertains more generally to self-assessment and to controlling our own learning. In the paragraphs that follow, we discuss each of these categories of strategies.

Noting Important Information

When students read, they often do so without much conscious effort. When they finish reading, however, they may have little to show for it. That is, they may find that they have comprehended very little. Some general strategies are useful for finding and capturing relevant content. Among the strategies that students use are: underlining (or highlighting) and note taking (Weinstein & Mayer, 1986). Although nearly 97 percent of postsecondary students claim to use underlining or highlighting while reading and studying (Caverly, Orlando, & Mullen, 2000), researchers question whether underlining is an effective learning strategy. For example, when investigating underlining among middle-school students, Kapinus and Haynes (1983) found that underlining was not useful for students with limited background knowledge of the topic. Essentially, students with lower levels of knowledge had difficulty differentiating important from trivial information. By comparison, underlining actually hindered the performance of good readers.

The question becomes, why do people underline or highlight? Our students are quite attached to the practice. Anderson and Armbruster (1984) found that underlining and highlighting gave students a sense of control over the content. Essentially, students believe that by underlining and highlighting they are actually monitoring their reading and studying the content. By highlighting particular lines or paragraphs, students feel that they will know what to reread when it comes time for the test. The mediating factor in this equation seems

Table 5.2   Toolbox of General Learning and Study Strategies

Capturing and Retaining Information	
Underlining or Highlighting	While reading a book, Bill underlines the information he believes is important.
Note Taking	In order to focus her attention on her reading assignment, Jolene writes down the information she reads and believes is important.
Information Search	While engaged in Jigsaw, a group technique, each student must search text documents and the Internet for relevant materials on his or her assigned topic.
Questioning	While reading the "Rivers of Ireland" chapter in her geography book, Jessica writes down questions that she would like to raise later during class discussion.
Improving Memory	
Rehearsal	In order to learn his phone number, Max, a kindergarten student, repeats it to himself many times.
Sorting and Categorizing	Chris participates in a game at a birthday party to see who can remember the most items on a tray after looking at them for a short time. He classifies the objects into categories such as "objects used in games" or "things you would take to the beach" to help remember them.
Mnemonics	To help her students remember the Circle of 5ths for her music theory class, Ms. Edwards taught them the phrase, "Fat Cats Go Down Alleys Eating Birds," because the first letter of each word corresponds to the next key in the circle.
Method of Loci	Juan needs to buy a few things from the store but can't find a pen to make a list. Instead, he pictures all the rooms of his house, with one necessary item placed in each room. When he arrives at the store, he mentally walks through his house to remember the needed items.
Analogical Reasoning	A teacher may help her young students learn to think about relationships between concepts by presenting them with analogies, such as King: Queen:: Prince: _____.
Comprehending and Recalling Text	
Identifying Important Ideas	Patty tries to pick out the main idea of every paragraph she reads.
Predicting	Before reading the end of the mystery novel, Elke tries to figure out "whodunit."
Summarizing	To make sure he can remember its important details, Robert tries to write a new abstract for the article he just read.

Comprehending and Recalling Text

Clarifying	Marcia talks herself through a portion of a chapter she is having a difficult time comprehending as a way to promote her comprehension.
Elaborating	While studying for an important exam, two students explain the concepts learned to one another, providing as many details and examples as they can.

Organizing Information

Outlining	Felix wants to make sure he has all the important information from a lecture in his notebook. Because the professor's lectures are very sequential and organized, Felix creates an outline so that he can use the hierarchical structure of the lecture during his studying.
Conceptual Mapping	In order to think about the relation between concepts she has been learning, Norma writes down all the concepts and draws lines between the concepts that are related.

Motivating Performance

Goal Setting	Before Rachel begins each new grading period, she sets particular goals for herself in terms of the level of performance she expects of herself.
Positive Self-Talk	During a grueling swim practice, Alec tells himself, "I can do this. I can finish these laps. I can go faster than I am now."
Self-Rewarding	Corinne decides that she will buy herself the new blouse she has been looking at after she finishes her term paper.

Monitoring and Regulating Learning

Task Analysis	Liam has to complete a large project for school. In order to begin, he determines the exact activities that must be done, as well as how long each will take to complete.
Self-Analysis	After reviewing the assignment for her creative writing class, Emma asks herself if she feels confident in completing the assignment or if she should ask the teacher some questions before beginning.
Help Seeking	Roberto asks the teacher and other students for help when he does not understand how to balance the equations in his chemistry class.
Formative Self-Evaluation	In the midst of writing his physics lab report, Scott asks himself if he is completing the calculations correctly and what he could do to help himself.

to be the extent to which students think deeply about the content they are marking.

Note taking, another strategy that may have limited effectiveness, is also used to capture information. What we do know is that the quantity and quality of students' class notes relate to their achievement (Kierwa, 1989). Unfortunately, the data also suggest that many students lack sufficient knowledge or the desire to take good notes (Anderson & Armbruster, 1986), and strategies like note taking, highlighting, and underlining are rarely taught in any explicit or formal way. Indeed, it seems that most students learn to take notes or highlight through vicarious modeling. Nonetheless, if students are going to routinely rely on underlining and note taking as information-gathering strategies, teachers should provide students with relevant declarative, procedural, and conditional knowledge concerning their use.

Organizing Information

Another technique students need is the ability to organize bodies of information (e.g., section of a textbook or class notes). Outlining, whether formal or informal, is perhaps the most common example of this type of strategy (Caverly et al., 2000). *Outlines* are essentially hierarchical organizations that tell us at a glance which ideas are overarching and which are supportive. Although there is no need to be rigorous in the use of outlining conventions (e.g., always having two supporting statements under each major heading) to capture the basic structure of text, it seems important that students be able to delineate the structure of the text.

Concept maps can also be used as a mechanism for understanding the organization of the text. A *concept map* is a schematic representation of information that also indicates the interrelation of the concepts displayed. Research on concept maps indicates that they are useful in enhancing students' comprehension and recall of text, as well as students' ability to indicate the relative importance of ideas in text (Romance & Vitale, 1992).

In classrooms, outlining and concept mapping are quite common forms of general learning and study strategies. Moreover, these forms of organizational learning and studying strategies have been shown to be beneficial (Romance & Vitale, 1992). Those benefits are not equally distributed, however. Specifically, when Caverly and colleagues (2000) surveyed the research on outlining and mapping, they found that students of low to average reading ability significantly improved their learning and studying when taught to outline or map.

On the other hand, high-ability students did not find much benefit to mapping. It seems that such a strategy may not be necessary for these students and instead becomes distracting.

Two important suggestions have surfaced in research on organizational strategies (Caverly et al., 2000). Without instruction, only high-ability students benefit from these organizational strategies. As such, students need to be explicitly taught outlining and mapping strategies. Second, organizational strategies like outlining and mapping cannot compensate for a lack of relevant knowledge. This means that students cannot effectively outline or map if they are not also provided with some base of knowledge about the subject matter.

Memory Bolsters

Remembering is fundamental to learning. It is difficult to think deeply about the Kreb's cycle if you cannot remember the steps or processes involved. Indeed, the ability to remember remains one of the potent differences between academically successful and unsuccessful students (Badderly, 1982). Fortunately there are strategies that can help us increase the quantity and quality of what we remember. For example, when people try to memorize long numbers (e.g., phone number or a street address), they often employ a memory strategy called chunking (Ellis & Hunt, 1983). *Chunking* is the process of breaking information into meaningful units that can be more easily recalled. For instance, a common chunking technique taught in elementary school is sorting or categorizing. By sorting and categorizing objects into groups, it is easier for students to remember the individual items in the group (Gaskill & Murphy, 2004). The research on how students process information has shown that students' mental capacities would quickly become overloaded were it not for chunking (Miller, 1956).

Individuals born in the 20th century are not the first to discover memory strategies. In fact, ancient Greek orators used such strategies as method of loci to remember extensive speeches (Goetz, Alexander, & Ash, 1992).

Another class of memory techniques used frequently, especially in schools, is mnemonics. A *mnemonic* is a memory trick in which some word, phrase, or even picture comes to represent a large body of information (Levin, 1993). For example, individuals use the popular first-letter mnemonic HOMES to remember the names of the Great Lakes (i.e., Huron, Ontario, Michigan, Erie, and Superior). There is also the sentence mnemonic "My Very Excellent Mother Just Served

Us Nine Pizzas" to remember the nine planets in order (i.e., Mercury, Venus, Earth, Mars, Jupiter, Saturn, Uranus, Neptune, and Pluto).

Strategies That Motivate

You do not have to sit in a classroom long before you realize that not everything is innately interesting. Indeed, sometimes even teachers get bored. Nonetheless, if teachers are teaching more about less and teaching principles and content knowledge, then there is a high probability that there will be content in which students have no interest but still need to learn. As Alexander (1997b) has suggested, much of schooling is spent in unfamiliar and nonstimulating territory. Yet, as we know all too well, administrators, teachers, and students must all be able to persist at tasks that are not intrinsically interesting. There are a number of strategies that students can use to help motivate themselves. Goal setting is one such motivating strategy. By setting overall goals and subgoals, students have a sense of how they are progressing at a certain task. Essentially, these goals become benchmarks against which learners can mark their progress.

"I can do it." Motivating Self-Talk

Much of being able to accomplish a task is knowing and believing that you can do it. In Chapter 4, we referred to this type of motivational belief as self-efficacy. It seems that believing you can do a task is extremely motivating (Bandura, 1977). As Vygotsky (1934) taught us, self-talk or self-speech is very important in learning and development. These internal conversations help us reflect and solve problems. Unfortunately, people are generally much better at destroying their confidence than they are at building themselves up. For instance, Chiu and Alexander (2000) studied preschoolers' private speech as they engaged in various physical (e.g., jumping) and mental (e.g., puzzle completion) tasks. They found that some children manifested positive self-talk (e.g., "I can do this. I am a good jumper."), while others were more negative in their private speech (e.g., "This is too far. I won't make it."). We would argue that most of this type of self-deprecating talk is learned through direct or vicarious modeling. Children hear teachers and parents say things like this about themselves or even directly to children, and children take on that belief. What is most important to remember is that students of all ages are impressionable, and the more that administrators and teachers employ positive self-talk when they are around students, the better students tend to do on the various tasks.

Determining the Prize

Like positive self-talk, self-rewarding is an example of self-reinforcement, providing yourself with some form of positive consequence after you have accomplished a particular goal or subgoal (Woolfolk, 2001). Some self-rewards are small and may include treating oneself to a latte or taking a brisk walk on a pretty day. Such rewards are quite appropriate for meeting subgoals. When you reach an overall goal or a larger subgoal (e.g., writing an entire chapter versus a section of a chapter), you need to self-reward accordingly.

For adults, the rewards are probably going to be different from what they are for students. For example, for each subgoal met, a middle-schooler might play 20 minutes of video games. When they accomplish the whole task, they might use their allowance to buy a new video game. The "reward" must come from the student and be suitable to the accomplishment. Negative consequences can occur when students' performance is tied to external rewards set by others, as when parents pay their children for grades (Pintrich & Schunk, 2001). In addition, the reward must come after the task is completed. If the reward is given in anticipation of task completion, then there is a possibility that the individual will lose motivation.

Self-Assessment: You Be the Judge

As students learn to self-motivate and self-reward, they must also learn how to judge their own performance accurately (Maehr & Anderman, 1993). By teaching students to self-assess, they will not be so dependent on the opinions or evaluations of teachers and parents to tell them if they have done well or poorly (Zimmerman & Martinez-Pons, 1992). It is not that the evaluations of teachers or parents are not important. Rather, it is extremely useful for students to be able to monitor and evaluate their own progress during the course of completing a task. Good strategic thinkers develop an internal gauge that tells them when they must come off autopilot, and good strategic thinkers are continually monitoring these internal gauges. Thus, they are quick to act when a slight glitch in performance occurs because they are self-monitoring and self-regulating (Winne, 1995). Researchers often use the term *metacognition* to describe this process of reflecting on and evaluating one's own thoughts and learning. Metacognition essentially means thinking about thinking (Garner, 1987).

The ability to self-regulate and self-monitor does not come easily, and many aspects of these processes develop over time (Winne, 1995;

Zimmerman, 1995). In some ways, it is a matter of having suitable learning experiences and building on these experiences. Thus, with each passing year, good strategic thinkers become increasingly better at analyzing academic tasks and better able to assess their own strengths and weaknesses relative to those tasks (Graham & Weiner, 1996). For example, the students whom Gaskill and Murphy (2004) taught to sort and categorize should become better at seeing the relations among concepts, words, or objects with continued exposure and practice. As they progress and develop, they should thus be better equipped to apply memory strategies such as chunking more effectively.

Help Seeking

A vital aspect of self-monitoring and self-regulating is knowing when to seek help (Harris & Graham, 1996). The interesting aspect of seeking help is that some types of help seeking can signal adaptive behavior, while other forms of help seeking signal maladaptive behavior. Intelligent use of this strategy is what McCaslin and Good (1996) refer to as "adaptive" help seeking. To grasp the difference between adaptive and maladaptive help seeking, we can contrast the behavior of two high-school students who are working together on a task, Dewey and Paige. If Dewey has come to rely too heavily and too often on Paige to get him through biology assignments, this would suggest that his help seeking is maladaptive. Paige, on the other hand, has learned to ask for assistance only when the situation warrants.

Good strategic thinkers like Paige make reasoned choices about when to turn to others for assistance. They are equally thoughtful about whom they choose as helpers. Although teachers are often the first persons whom students turn to when seeking assistance, peers can be excellent sources of help in school learning (McCaslin & Good, 1996). In fact, if teachers fashion themselves as but one source of credibility, as discussed in Chapter 3, then students will more readily seek help from other students. If Dewey worked to develop a base of biology knowledge, and knew how to work more collaboratively with Paige, then she could prove to be an excellent ally, given her knowledge and interest in science. To encourage this type of strategic behavior, we often suggest that our college students seek out those who seem to be achieving good grades and see if they can form a study group with these individuals.

The difficulty, however, is that help seeking often has negative connotations associated with it. Many students, especially those in the younger grades, believe that help seeking is a sign of incompetence, and older students think seeking help is simply not "cool." In fact, Newman and Goldin (1990) found that 70 percent of the 3rd graders they asked felt that the dumb or stupid kids in their classroom were more apt to seek help. Although older students may not think it is "cool" to seek help, they seem to also realize that the students who do seek help are usually the very same individuals who perform well in classrooms.

This is probably why Newman and Goldin found that 60 percent of the 7th graders surveyed felt that the "smart" students in their classes were those who asked for help, often by questioning their teachers. McCaslin and Good (1996) believe administrators and teachers can have a tremendous influence in creating learning environments that foster adaptive help-seeking behavior. Rather than discouraging students from turning to other students when problems arise, students should be explicitly taught how and when to seek help, as well as from whom to seek help.

Navigating the Nuance of Strategic Processing

Often, what separates good from poor learners is their strategic ability. Good strategic thinkers can easily be differentiated from poor strategic thinkers (Weinstein & Mayer, 1986). Essentially, good strategic thinkers possess a well-equipped strategy toolbox, and they know exactly what strategic tool will fit the current situation (Alexander, 1997b). Individuals who possess a vast repertoire of general strategies that they can apply to novel tasks have been referred to as *intelligent novices* (Brown & Campione, 1990).

What sets these types of individuals apart, whether administrator, teacher, or student, is the fact that they are self-regulating. The ability to self-regulate requires knowledge, motivation, and strategic processing ability. In essence, the ability to self-regulate is not something that one can acquire immediately. Rather, as discussed in Chapter 2, self-regulatory behavior must be honed and refined with every learning experience.

Moreover, self-regulatory behavior must be modeled and rewarded in rich learning environments. For example, learners must believe that they can accomplish what they set out to do in a particular domain (Sternberg, 1985). They must possess a high sense of self-efficacy for the task or problem (Pintrich & Schunk, 2001). In addition, learners must dedicate a great deal of time and energy toward establishing a base of relevant subject-matter knowledge, including a body of general and domain-specific strategies (Alexander, 1997b). Competency does not just happen. It must be sought and worked toward. Strategic learning, just like strategic teaching, is effortful. Students must also acquire a personal interest in a field if they are to keep their drive toward competence alive (Alexander & Murphy, 1998a).

One of the difficulties that this presents for teachers is that the truly self-regulatory student will most likely not be equally invested in every content area. As a result, it may be that a student chooses to spend a tremendous amount of time studying and learning mathematics but barely completes her assignment for English literature. For some administrators and teachers, this presents a troubling situation. It is not that we think it is good practice for students to pass only the course they like, but rather we think it is important for teachers to realize that truly self-regulatory behavior manifests in ways that may not be in line with our traditional notion of schooling. Another difficulty is that when not challenged, high-knowledge students do not require strategies to achieve, and therefore do not need to show much effort on certain tasks (Alexander & Murphy, 1998a). For good reason, educators and educational leaders, especially in elementary schools, want to see students putting a great deal of effort into learning tasks.

Based on our own research, we would suggest that teachers instruct students to follow the old adage to "work smarter, not harder" (Weinstein & Mayer, 1986). Essentially, with good instruction, students can construct a base of relevant knowledge, articulate reasonable goals, and make sound judgments about their capabilities (Fuchs et al., 2003). In effect, the students will be responsible for using their knowledge and strategic abilities to blaze their own trails toward academic development—trails that reflect their academic strengths, personal interests, values, and perceived competencies.

What Principles Can Instructional Leaders Employ to Promote Students' Strategic Behavior?

One overarching issue in this chapter is that effective learning demands effective strategic thinking. Another is that students who do not possess a sufficient repertoire of general and domain-specific strategies are doomed to wander through their school years, and perhaps life, in an aimless and precarious manner. Unfortunately, too many students never acquire the strategic wherewithal to benefit from their educational experiences. Those lucky enough or skilled enough to construct their own strategic arsenals move efficiently through the academic landscape (Paris et al., 1991).

The important question that remains is: What can administrators and teachers do to encourage strategic thinking in their students? What guidelines should administrators and teachers follow to create learning environments that foster rather than hinder successful, adaptive strategic processes? Teachers can do a great deal to help their students become better thinkers and problem solvers by teaching in such a way as to enhance the strategic thinking that occurs in the learning environment.

- ## Strategic thinking must be demonstrated and modeled

For administrators, teachers, and their students, the proof that strategies work lies in the success they engender. It is one thing to tell students that strategies make a significant difference in their learning and performance but quite another to demonstrate the power of strategic processing. By demonstrating chunking and sorting, Gaskill and Murphy (2004) successfully modeled the process of grouping information in meaningful ways that resulted in better memory. Through this experiment, the children could not help but see the effect of chunking for themselves. With that personal realization, students are far more likely to apply the strategies learned in other learning situations.

Because this chapter is more focused on student learning than managing the learning environment, we will not discuss the vast literatures on instructional strategies (e.g., teachers' strategies for grouping students) or classroom management strategies (e.g., responding to inattentive students). However, the same principles directed toward learning and studying can also apply to these forms of strategic processing. For example, as with the successful use of learning and instructional strategies, the effective use of instructional and classroom management strategies is enhanced by their modeling by administrators and master teachers.

- ## Strategic thinking must be paired with explicit instruction

The simple fact is that many individuals go successfully through life without explicit strategy instruction. We are often surprised to discover how many of our bright and capable students manage to get so far in their education with only limited strategies. The unfortunate reality is that the vast majority of these college students have never been explicitly taught strategies for studying or for complex problem solving. This situation often causes us to question how much better learners these individuals could be if they used relevant general and domain-specific strategies. The situation seems analogous for kindergarten through high school, in that there are many students who could be much better learners if they possessed strategy knowledge. Surely, explicit strategy instruction would enhance their abilities (Spencer, Scruggs, & Mastropieri, 2003) when they were provided with ample opportunities to apply those strategies in meaningful and challenging contexts.

Among the strategies that Alexander (e.g., Alexander, Murphy, & Kulikowich, 1998) often teaches her undergraduates are steps for solving classical analogies, much like the ones they have encountered on standardized aptitude and achievement exams (e.g., HERD : COW :: FLOCK : ?; Goswami, 1992; Sternberg, 1977). Interestingly, her students are usually quite confident that they have performed well on the analogy task. For instance, a teacher might present the following problem:

OCEAN : BAY :: CONTINENT : _____

The students quickly and confidently fill in the blanks with such words as country, countries, island, and nation. They are then dismayed to learn that none of these words is the *preferred* response. Given that this item uses rather commonplace terms, students are convinced that they do really know how to process such problems. Rather, their errors are indicative of their lack of knowledge about analogical reasoning.

With explicit instruction, students recognize that they may not have analyzed each term in the problem deeply (i.e., encode). For example, a bay is a body of water that extends off the ocean and is surrounded by land on three sides. Or, they may have failed to form the critical relations between ocean and bay (i.e., infer), ocean and continent (i.e., map), or between bay and the missing term. If they had, they would have realized that "peninsula" fits all these relations best, since it is a body of land that extends off a continent and is surrounded by water on three sides.

It is important that those who wish to teach strategically must reflect on strategies and the processes underlying them. Then, they must make this knowledge public so their students can use it (Paris et al., 1991). That is the only way teachers can be sure their students are at least exposed to the elements of good strategic thinking.

- **Integrate strategy instruction with content in ways that are meaningful and practical**

When many of us were in elementary school, the transition and integration of content across subject matters were, at best, sketchy. For example, you can probably recall situations in science or history, where you *read* an entire chapter of your textbook and then the teacher would say some thing like: "Okay, put your science books away. It is time to do *reading*." Although teachers are aware that their lesson content also involves reading, they do not make that connection explicit for their students. The same thing can happen with strategy instruction. If strategy instruction is to be effective, administrators should encourage teachers to explicate in their lesson plans how the strategic threads weave throughout the content.

In essence, strategic thinking should be infused in the content and activities of the classroom and across subject domains. For example, we should introduce the idea of finding the main idea not only in reading class but whenever students encounter such a task that is relevant in their content courses. The same could be said of situations in which an administrator might want to instruct teachers on new instructional or management strategies. That is, such instruction should be embedded in relevant content. Artificiality in either the setting or the context will often work against students' ability to see a strategy as truly fundamental to their learning (Sternberg & Wagner, 1986).

An important aspect of infusing strategic thinking into the classroom community begins with the language and concepts teachers use during instruction. Teachers should find opportunities to introduce terms like *compare, predict,* and *cause/effect* in their interactions with students (Perkins, 1992). As we will discuss in Chapter 6, teachers could easily accomplish this as a component of group discourse or even as a mechanism for informal assessment of students' understandings. For example, if a teacher asks her 1st graders to compare a picture on page 6 of their reading book with a picture on page 10, she might remind the children of strategies that can be used in comparing the pictures. The point is that teachers should take time to explain, reinforce, or elaborate on strategies and processes that they feel will aid students in learning and thinking when the strategies seem facilitative (Garner, 1990).

- **Strategic competence begins with just a few strategies**

Based on his own extensive line of research on strategic processing, Pressley and colleagues (1989) recommend that teachers be selective in the number of strategies they teach at any given time. As was the case with content knowledge, Pressley recommends teaching more about less when it comes to strategies—at least when building a repertoire of strategies. If teachers will teach only a few strategies at one time and cover them well, then students will be able to personalize the strategies and transfer them to other tasks.

For example, Pressley has suggested the four basic text processing strategies that are part of the Reciprocal Teaching Model devised by Palincsar and Brown (1984) as candidates for initial strategy instruction. As discussed in Chapter 6, teachers can focus on the general strategies of questioning, predicting, clarifying, and summarizing and infuse them throughout the curriculum. Once these strategies are well understood and broadly practiced by students in diverse contexts, teachers can move on to other strategies.

Our caveat to Pressley's recommendation, however, is that teachers must be alert to those strategic moments when the teaching of a new or alternative strategy would closely parallel the class problem or assignment. Understandably, however, those new strategies will remain fragile knowledge until students have repeated practice with and exposure to them. Further, due to variation across grades, content, and students, there is no perfectly applicable "starter set" of strategies. Perhaps a high-school shop/mechanics teacher would find that certain general and domain-specific strategies would be most beneficial to his students, while a middle-school art teacher might choose another set of initial strategies. Yet administrators should encourage teachers to teach new strategies with familiar content whenever possible and to use more complex or novel content with familiar strategies. By incorporating the new and old in this manner, administrators and teachers are more likely to avoid the problem of cognitive overload in their students, while enhancing the likelihood of transfer (i.e., applying what is known in new or unfamiliar contexts).

For example, Ms. Brian, a middle-school language arts teacher, often had her students construct concept maps before writing as a way to organize their thoughts and improve the final product. Mr. Taber, the social studies teacher at the same school, was frustrated with his students' inability to write a coherent extended response on his assignments and tests. The principal, Mrs. Kupp, suggested that Ms. Brian share her mapping strategy with Mr. Taber since it had proven to be effective for her and might work well for his students' difficulties in writing extended responses. Mrs. Kupp also felt that it would be particularly wise to show students at the school how they could use the same strategy for different kinds of writing tasks in different subject areas. After Ms. Brian worked with Mr. Taber, he was able to teach his students the concept mapping strategy as a pre-writing activity. Mr. Taber began to see an improvement in his students' writing almost immediately and planned to reinforce the strategy throughout the remainder of the school year.

- ## Students' strategic effort must be prompted, scaffolded, and rewarded

Like finicky tomato plants that have to be planted halfway up the stem to even have a chance at growing, strategies need care and maintenance. Students' internalization and adoption of those strategies will remain fragile knowledge for some time, regardless of how well those strategies are initially taught. As such, it is important for teachers to remind students to apply their strategic knowledge either by prompting or cueing. Some researchers have even encouraged the use of explicit checklists in strategy training (Harris & Graham, 1996). In addition, as Harris and Graham have suggested, this type of checklist can also be used to promote self-regulation and monitoring through self-assessment.

It should not be assumed that checklists can completely replace guidance and support from teachers (e.g., teacher modeling, questioning, or probing). For the teacher, this type of guidance serves two purposes. For one, the teacher will be able to detect aspects or steps of strategies that need to be retaught or reinforced. In addition, teachers can use such opportunities to introduce new content or informally quiz students on old content. The teacher might also find it useful to have students demonstrate how they are performing a particular task or applying a given strategy. Teachers can gather valuable insights by watching as students solve problems using strategies.

Finally, teacher modeling and reinforcing strategies will help create an environment that fosters strategic process. Research suggests that students—especially young and less able students—are non-strategic in their thinking and learning, in part because the learning environment does not offer sufficient time or opportunity to think and act strategically (Garner, 1990). For example, there are also no clear rewards for the students who employ strategies on "fill-in-the-blank" assessments. Such concerns may become exacerbated as teachers feel the increased pressure to "cover the content" or to "teach to the test." The fact is that performing strategically takes more time than simply operating on autopilot. What's more is that students who are acting strategically need time to explore alternative possibilities and conclusions. Thus, as Garner (1990) deduced, even though many school administrators and teachers *say* they want students to be more strategic, they do not really want to deal with the potential consequences of strategic thinking.

- **Encourage the self in strategic thinking, such as goals, personalization, self-regulation, and self-assessment**

Strategic processing must involve the learner as an active participant. The learners must take ownership of a given strategy. The students must regulate their ability to use the strategy through the process of self-assessment. Indeed, good strategic thinkers adopt a "self-as-agent" perspective and understand that they have a large measure of control over their learning and development (Winne, 1995). Strategic teachers contribute directly and purposefully to this perception of self-as-agent. However, administrators and teachers must help students take charge of their learning and development. Merely handing over the reins to young or naïve learners will not create the desired outcome (Graves, 1997). Transfer of responsibility to learners should be progressive and gradual and accomplished in a learning environment that addresses strategic thinking in an explicit and integrated manner. In essence, administrators who want their teachers to be successful at promoting strategic thinking in their students must be willing to allow them to spend a great deal of time and energy setting the groundwork for self-as-agent.

Chapter Reflections

As effective administrators and master teachers realize, effective learning demands effective strategic thinking. Moreover, quality administrators and teachers understand that they play a primary role in guiding their students toward better strategic thinking. Strategies, as we have discussed, entail far more than the kinds of skills that students acquire in the natural course of everyday living. To be competent in learning, students should acquire an array of both general and domain-specific strategies.

In this chapter, we also set out to answer the question of whether there are basic strategies that are tied to academic success. In answering this question, we saw that there are a range of general and specific strategies important to academic performance. As such, we surmised that effective learners must be knowledgeable and competent in many general and domain-specific strategies—strategies that must be differentially applied given the context of the domain, problem, and situation.

In this discussion, we also focused on the principles guiding the development and manifestation of strategic thinking in classroom environments. Specifically, we surveyed six guidelines that can help educators and educational leaders become models of strategic teaching. For example, administrators and teachers must be models and demonstrators of strategic behaviors and take time to make strategy instruction an explicit part of the school curriculum. In addition, administrators and teachers should concentrate on a few strategies at a time that are meaningfully and practically integrated into the content. We also suggested that good strategic teaching should place importance on the prompting or scaffolding of students' strategic efforts. Moreover, students need support and guidance from their school administrators and classroom teachers in the form of prompts and cues. In addition, learning environments that encourage strategic thinking are places where the self is given prominence—students are guided toward self-regulating, self-monitoring, and self-assessment. Collectively, these research-based guidelines can do much to make strategic learning a reality in the classroom.

TOURO COLLEGE LIBRARY

6

Harnessing the Power of Shared Learning

Guiding Questions

- What is meant by shared learning?
- Are there approaches to shared learning that promote achievement?
- How can instructional leaders promote shared learning in classrooms?

What Is Meant by Shared Learning?

Despite the fact that most educational assessments are measures of individual achievement, learning can also be characterized as a social process. In essence, the process of becoming educated in schools requires human interaction in a stimulating and supporting social environment (Alexander & Murphy, 1998b). Because schools are social institutions, learning is fundamentally a socially shared enterprise in which culturally valued content is shared (Cole, Gay, Glick, & Sharp, 1971). Further, classrooms are microcosms within the larger social enterprise of schools. It is within the classroom context that the thoughts, ideas, and actions of one individual are reciprocally influenced by the thoughts, ideas, and actions of others (Bandura, 1986).

The Benefits of Shared Learning

One implication of this presupposition is that understanding cannot be thought of as the sole property of any one person but is essentially distributed among all the individuals within a given classroom and school (Hastie & Pennington, 1991). Conceptualized in this way, the socially shared and socially distributed nature of schooling is quite evident.

In addition, learning is necessarily a situated and contextualized enterprise. Learning happens at a specific time and in a specific place, and the characteristics of that time and place matter greatly in how students learn and develop (Wertsch, 1985). Decisions made jointly by administrators and teachers to integrate content, for instance, are different from learning each content area separately. Indeed, there is more to these environments than the behavioral notion of stimuli and response. There is also more to these environments than a set of cognitive inputs and outputs. Like the process of learning itself, educational environments are fluid, social, dynamic, and reciprocal (Alexander & Murphy, 1998b). In recent years, the social and contextual dimensions of learning have taken on new importance (Wertsch, 1985). Today, most educational researchers and experienced educators understand how important it is for teachers to build effective learning environments that take advantage of the social and contextual character of human learning and development (Brown, Collins, & Duguid, 1989).

However, taking advantage of the social learning environment requires that students and teachers be social with each other. The contemporary practice of encouraging students to be social, even about content, is a substantive divergence from the practices of years past. Such a change requires a tremendous commitment both by administrators and teachers—a change to a system in which educators relinquish some control of the classroom environment. A classroom embracing the social nature of learning would replace past management models, which virtually set out to eliminate or constrain any student-to-student interactions in the classroom for the sake of order. Rather, through professional development, many administrators have helped teachers replace such ideas with models that promote verbal exchanges and shared thinking between teachers and students (Cazden, 1988; Mehan, 1979). Requisite to this educational transformation are administrators and teachers who can relinquish archaic notions that the teacher should be the *sole* source and disseminator of relevant academic content (Kantor, Green, Bradley, & Lin, 1992). In classrooms embracing the social, students are encouraged to raise questions and seek knowledge, and are responsible for becoming partners in establishing the agenda of the classroom (Lemke, 1990; Palincsar & Brown, 1984).

Although many theorists and researchers have studied the roles of situation and context in learning, few have been as influential as Lev Vygotsky (1978). One of Vygotsky's most influential concepts was the zone of proximal development (ZPD). The ZPD is a simple but powerful principle. Simply stated, when individuals are assisted by more knowledgeable or experienced teachers or peers, their potential for learning is markedly greater than it would be if they were working independently (Loentiev, 1981; Scrimsher & Tudge, 2003). The more knowledgeable "other" serves as a support system that helps the student achieve. The distance between assisted and independent thinking is referred to as the "zone" in the ZPD. Multiple factors influence the ZPD, including the familiarity or complexity of the task and the effectiveness of the support or guidance. The fundamental principle of the ZPD is the cornerstone of many of the instructional techniques discussed in this chapter.

Shared Learning Versus Competition

American schools can be characterized as somewhat competitive in nature. Shared learning is most often thought of as an alternative to competitive educational models (Deutsch, 1949; Heath, 1991). *Competition* refers to an educational approach in which teachers assess student performance by a comparison to others (Slavin, 1995). In such a system, performance gains are determined not only by what the student does but also by the performance of other students. In such a system, achievement becomes contingent on the level of performance of others within the comparison or norming group (McCaslin & Good, 1996; Webb & Palincsar, 1996). Recent initiatives in the United States are expanding the types of competitive systems beyond the classroom to the school and school district level by tying funding to normative achievement gains. In such a system, the reality is that an individual or school can attain its goal only if other participants do not obtain theirs (Graham & Weiner, 1996, p. 79).

Some have argued that competition is a reality of life (McCaslin & Good, 1996). Others have argued that competition can be a motivating factor that encourages students to make even greater achievement gains (Oakes, 1990). Despite such support, the potential side effects of competition have been well established. In fact, competitive and cooperative learning approaches have been compared for over 50 years. This work has demonstrated that competition increases anxiety, lowers students' self-esteem, limits creativity, creates negative feelings among classmates, and can even make students feel less responsible for their classmates' success or well-being (Deutsch, 1949, 1993). Researchers in the field of motivation have delineated similar problems with competitive systems (Pintrich & Schunk, 2001). Competition seems to foster unwanted or nonproductive behaviors (e.g., cheating), can be more problematic for females and for certain cultural groups, promotes performance goals over mastery goals, gives rise to causal attributions that stress ability over effort, and, unfortunately, translates into lower grades and less valuing of learning.

Although the reality is that competition will probably always be present in schools (Nicholls, 1989), administrators and teachers should think deeply about the negative consequences of this approach to learning. Certainly, for those working to build a sense of community in their schools and classrooms, competition should be downplayed. Teachers should generally avoid pitting students against one another for the sake of academic achievement (Pugach & Johnson, 1995).

Are There Approaches to Shared Learning That Promote Achievement?

As is the case with knowledge and motivation, the education literature is replete with terminology related to shared learning. It would behoove administrators and teachers who are interested in initiating or expanding shared learning experiences in their own schools and classrooms to be conversant with some of the most central terms. Each signifies some level of shared learning, and each can be found in some form in today's effective schools (Webb & Palincsar, 1996). The first step in orchestrating social interactions in classrooms and schools is to understand the language of socially shared learning. These definitions (see Table 6.1) will help you begin to understand the distinctions between cooperation and shared learning or to recognize alternative forms of cooperative learning.

Table 6.1   Definitions of Relevant Terms

Term	Definition	Example
Collaboration	Co-constructed understanding, where participants produce consensus or come to agreement on a given issue, response, or topic.	*In order to help students complete their mathematics homework, a teacher structures his class so that students may work collaboratively to determine the best answer to each of the problems.*
Competition	Performance assessed through comparison with the performance of others.	*Because the teacher of an advanced chemistry class assigns grades based on how students perform relative to their classmates, students scramble to obtain the highest grade possible on each assignment.*
Cooperation	Situations where students must work together to achieve a common goal.	*A teacher structures a cooperative learning activity so that each member of the team brings different information that all students will need in order to be successful in the activity.*
Discussion	Constructive conversations or verbal exchanges between students and teachers.	*In order to learn from each other and gain different perspectives, three teachers enrolled in a Masters-level course talk about how the issues discussed in class affect their classrooms.*
Real Questions Synonym: Authentic questions	Questions for which the answer is not known or assumed, or questions that participants find stimulating and worthy of exploration.	*During a discussion in a department meeting, an administrator asks the teachers how they feel the new curriculum is affecting their students' learning.*

Classroom Discussions

As we have suggested above, discussions are at the heart of social learning. We loosely define a *discussion* as a constructive conversation between students and teachers who are willing to listen and learn from one another (Lemke, 1990). What makes a quality discussion is not just that multiple speakers interject their individual thoughts and ideas, but that those ideas become intertwined and interwoven together as shared understanding (Jetton & Alexander, 2000). Social psychologists who study group dynamics and communication see discussion as an invaluable educational tool that can occur with the whole classroom, a small group, or even in dyads (Mishler, 1978; Phillips, 1973). Moreover, discussions can be used to achieve several outcomes, including to: (a) help students explore the personal relevance of issues or content; (b) make students more active participants in the learning process; (c) put greater responsibility for learning on students' shoulders; (d) improve social skills; (e) promote comprehension; and (f) give teachers clues as to what students think or believe. Yet, if discussions are to achieve these laudable ends, teachers must understand certain basic principles of human communication that underlie effective verbal interchanges.

Rules Lead to Goals

Anyone who has spent time in classrooms appreciates how difficult it is to foster quality discussions. In many cases, teachers dominate classroom discussions so that they are sure to cover the content and so that students do not spread misconceptions (Murphy et al., 2004). The good news is that if teachers establish rules *a priori*, this is far less likely to happen. Teachers cannot expect students, who have spent most of their time in traditional classrooms, to know how to engage in a meaningful discussion instinctively (Jetton, 1994; Luft, 1970). Students must acquire good discussion skills through teacher explanation, modeling, and guided practice (Lipman, 1991).

Discussion rules should be somewhat simple and should be linked to the goals or purpose of the discussion. Students must know and abide by simple rules of acceptable conduct during discussions. While usually small in number, the discussion rules are closely adhered to during any class discussion and are often restated as the discussion begins. Rules may include some of the following: listen carefully; make your ideas known; support your opinions; one person speaks at a time; show mutual respect; participate but do not dominate; look at the person you are talking to and speak directly to them; offer constructive counterarguments; and remember to disagree with ideas, not other students. Many of these rules allow the teacher to become a participant in the discussion rather than the focal point of the discussion.

Good Questions Promote Good Discussions

Another key to good discussions are good questions. Almost all of the discussion approaches in the literature begin with some sort of question (Murphy et al., 2004). Sometimes the question is a central or defining one (Anderson et al., 1977). At other times discussion begins with a lower-level question about a topic (Palincsar & Brown, 1984). What is most important is that the question be real. A *real question*, or what Nystrand (2003) termed an "authentic" question, is one for which the answer is not already known or one the questioner is genuinely interested in exploring. In other words, the answer is not pre-specified.

According to Nystrand (2003), almost all student questions can be assumed to be real by default. Quite frequently, real questions allow for a range of responses and generate several responses before another question is asked. In thinking of real questions, especially those that will frame the discussion, teachers must ensure that they are suitably controversial or open-ended (Phillips, 1973) and that there is room for multiple perspectives and ideas. Real questions usually require some justification of respondents' positions (Cohen, 1994). Questions should also be crafted so that students have sufficient knowledge and experience to bring to the discussion (Alexander & Jetton, 2003). Finally, the ages and backgrounds of students should be considered when crafting questions (Phillips, 1973). For example, a teacher must decide whether her 4th-grade class has enough background knowledge on the causes of the Civil War in order to engage in a productive discussion.

For instance, in accordance with No Child Left Behind guidelines, Mr. Lauer, an elementary principal, teamed with Dr. Friend, a professor from a nearby university, to help teachers learn to identify and ask clear, thought-provoking questions during class discussions. Both Mr. Lauer and Dr. Friend agreed that discussions were important pedagogical tools that were not being used as often or as effectively as they could be. During the professional development sessions on classroom discourse, teachers were given guidance on how to use questioning to initiate and maintain discussions around important concepts in the class readings or the lessons.

Mr. Lauer also had his teachers videotape a lesson, which he used to reinforce the ideas touched on during Dr. Friend's professional development sessions. He also continued to meet with teachers throughout the semester to discuss their progress in this area. Based on the data that Dr. Friend collected before and after this intervention, there was a significant improvement in the frequency and quality of teachers' questions and also a marked increase in the frequency and quality of students' questions—just what Mr. Lauer and Dr. Friend wanted to see happen.

Openness and Trust Are Requisite

It is vital that students feel as though they can express their honest views—not those that they feel will win teacher approval (Alexander et al., 1994). Because teachers remain the principal authorities and evaluators in the classroom, it makes sense that students want to gain their approval. If students believe that there is a "true" position or stance that their teacher wants promoted, then many will bend their own views to fit that preferred position. One way to avoid this type of situation is for teachers to avoid entering a discussion in too strong or direct a manner. Facilitating class discussions and controlling them are very different modes of operation. In facilitating a discussion, teachers would prompt student responses, seek clarification, and reflect on a stated opinion. It is a very different situation when teachers interject supporting examples or explanations that constrain the discussion. If teachers want to aid students during discussions, they should be very careful to offer general support that does not reveal their own views in any explicit way.

Discussions Should Be Flexibly Implemented

Discussions should not be thought of as the sole or primary mode of content delivery, despite their strengths in building shared understanding. The effectiveness of discussions rests on a breadth or depth of knowledge and adequate interest in the topic or issue. As such, we urge administrators and teachers to consider discussions to be a useful complement to other forms of social interaction.

Moreover, it is important to remember that discussions require flexibility in scheduling. That is, effective discussions do not always fall within precise time limits (Kagan & Kagan, 1994). In the elementary grades, it may mean that the discussion might carry over into time set aside for another subject matter. For middle- or high-school teachers, whose students change classes, it may mean carrying the discussion into the next session. When the discussion is carried over to another day, it may be necessary to take steps to preserve the flow of conversation (Webb, 1989).

In being flexible, it may also be necessary to modify the physical environment of the classroom. A classroom of students sitting in rows of desks, unable to see or engage others easily, is unlikely to promote deep, meaningful discussion. Simply put, the physical arrangement in the learning environment can reinforce or undermine the goal of promoting the social exchange of ideas among students. This may mean that teachers will have to try multiple different arrangements to find the one that works best for their students and their goals (Kagan & Kagan, 1994).

For example, to cope with her large high-school literature classes, a colleague, Tamara Jetton, uses an arrangement she calls "inner-outer circle." The students form two concentric circles with their desks. Those seated in the inner circle begin the discussion, while those on the outer circle observe or make notes. Then, when signaled, the students shift positions. Those seated to the outside move into the inner circle and carry on the discussion, making references to the issues and arguments their classmates have already put forward.

Everyone Has to Participate

Like other forms of social interactions, discussion is most effective when all participants feel they have a role and a voice (Fuchs, Fuchs, Mathes, & Simmons, 1997). In any classroom, there are some students who find it difficult to hold back so that others can share, and there are some students who find it hard to speak out during discussions. Finding appropriate ways to promote balanced student involvement is part of the learning curve when using discussion as an instructional technique. Whatever actions teachers take, they need to ensure that all students participate in some manner during discussions (Kagan & Kagan, 1994).

Cooperation

Cooperation, as conceived by most educators, is thought of as the opposite of competition (McCaslin & Good, 1996). We use the word *cooperation* to refer to situations in which students come together to work toward some common academic goal or end (Webb & Palincsar, 1996). Unlike competitive approaches, in a cooperative system each student's academic success depends to some degree on the success of his or her classmates.

There are many types of instructional approaches that fall within the category of cooperative learning. Several cooperative learning models are well researched and show positive learning outcomes (Johnson & Johnson, 1994, 1999; Johnson, Johnson, & Stanne, 2000). Given the space limitations, we will look at three of the well-researched approaches (i.e., Learning Together and Alone, Jigsaw, and Group

Investigation). We selected these three approaches, in part, because they are not as structured as other cooperative approaches. We made this decision because we wanted to focus on cooperative approaches that could be applied to a range of grades, ability levels, and content domains. While a number of the more structured cooperative approaches have been well researched (e.g., *Team Assisted Individualization;* Slavin, Leavey, & Madden, 1985), those approaches tend to be most useful with younger learners who are struggling to acquire basic skills in reading or mathematics.

Administrators should help their teachers interested in cooperative approaches to learning and development spend time exploring the various approaches. Additional cooperative approaches are overviewed in Table 6.2.

Learning Together and Alone

Johnson and Johnson are major advocates of cooperative learning, and their work has paved the way for the various cooperative approaches displayed in Table 6.2 (Johnson & Johnson, 1994, 1999; Johnson et al., 2000). Their model of cooperation is called Learning Together and Alone (LT). In the LT model, four or five students of differing abilities work together on carefully chosen assignments with clearly specified goals (Johnson & Johnson, 1999). The students work together in this group on the assignment and turn the product in as a group for feedback and evaluation. What the LT requires is that teachers spend a great deal of time doing team-building activities with student groups. The team-building activities allow the students to take on various roles in the group (e.g., reporter or questioner; Johnson & Johnson, 1994). Even if a teacher does not find the LT useful in a particular context or situation, it may be that the notion of cooperative student roles would still be useful. Kagan (1992) has devised an extensive list of cooperative learning roles, including cheerleader, coach, question commander, and material monitor. These kinds of roles can be modified and used with students of varying ages and in diverse situations.

Jigsaw

Aronson and colleagues (e.g., Aronson, 1978; Aronson, Blaney, Sikes, Stephan, & Snapp, 1978; Aronson & Patnoe, 1997) devised a cooperative learning approach that is useful for a variety of content areas, particularly with older students. In *Jigsaw*, the teacher chooses the topic or theme (e.g., story structure) and then breaks that topic into subtopics (e.g., plot, antagonists, protagonists, or climax). The

Table 6.2   Comparison of Well-Researched Cooperative Learning
Approaches

Cooperative Learning Approaches	
Approach	*Implementation*
Learning Together and Alone	• Four or five students of mixed ability work in groups. • Focuses on well-specified tasks. • Effective both with young learners and those in need of instruction on basic skills.
Student Teams-Achievement Divisions (STAD)	• Four or five students of mixed ability work in groups. • Tasks follow teacher's lessons and curriculum. • Effective in teaching and improving basic skills.
Team-Assisted Individualization (TAI)	• Pairs of students work together. • Tasks include programmed, individualized instructional materials. • Effective for individualized instruction and evaluation of well-structured problems.
Teams-Games-Tournament (TGT)	• Three students of similar achievement levels work in groups. • Tasks are specifically defined with group members rotating roles. • Effective in using competition and letting high-ability students work together.
Cooperative Integrated Reading and Composition (CIRC)	• Four students work in groups. • Focuses on a well-specified curriculum. • Effective in reading comprehension, writing mechanics, and spelling.
Jigsaw	• Four to six students of mixed ability work in both expert groups and home groups. • Works well with varied subject matter areas so that all students can become experts in a certain area. • Especially appropriate for older students.
Group Investigation	• Two to six groups of the students' choosing work together. • Content is specified by the students and approved by the teacher. • Effective in introducing student choice into the groups and the projects completed.

teacher then divides the class into groups, with approximately six
students, corresponding to the number of subtopics. Each team member
selects one of the subtopics to research independently, and the students

researching the same subtopic (e.g., plot) get together and share the results of their independent research. Once the students have completed their research, they return to their original, base group and serve as the "expert" on that subtopic. One of the key aspects of jigsaw is that it does not require much planning and can be quickly learned by students.

Group Investigation

Jigsaw is not the only method that is project-based. *Group Investigation* (GI) is a project-based cooperative technique in which students work together to complete a project they select (Sharan, 1994; Sharan & Sharan, 1992). What differentiates GI from Jigsaw is that students form their own groups of two to six. The role of the teacher is to facilitate the selection of the part or portion of the larger class project that the group would like to research. After completion, the group shares the results with the whole class. Like Jigsaw, this method is very flexible and easy to implement.

Collaboration

Collaborative learning is a special form of shared learning (Cohen, 1994). In *collaboration,* the idea is to foster shared thinking and learning to produce consensus or agreement among the participants on a given question, project, or topic. The outcome of such an exercise is essentially co-constructed understanding rather than an external product that is evaluated by others. As such, much of the collaborative activities focus on externalizing, confirming, clarifying, and acknowledging students' shared understandings. Herein, we discuss two prominent forms of collaborative learning (i.e., Reciprocal Teaching and Scripted Cooperation).

Reciprocal Teaching

Given that text remains a prominent form of learning material in classrooms, it was important to discuss one collaborative technique that focuses on text. *Reciprocal Teaching* (RT) is a text-based, collaborative instructional approach in which groups of students work together to make sense of texts from specific subject areas (Brown & Palincsar, 1987). Although RT begins as a teacher-led approach, the idea is that the teacher instructs students to become facilitators of their own groups, which makes RT unique among collaborative approaches. The actions of the group center on four comprehension strategies: summarizing, questioning, clarifying, and predicting.

Students try to capture the main idea of a text segment by answering the guiding question: "What is the author trying to say?" This is referred to as *summarizing*. The purpose of *questioning* is to explore the group's understanding of specific elements of text. For example, while discussing a passage on the American judicial system, the student facilitator might say: "What does the author mean by innocent until proven guilty?" The process of *clarifying* helps the group better understand confusing points in the text. A story on the seasons, for example, might elicit the question: "Why does seeing turkeys in August make the rancher think that winter is coming early?" Finally, *predicting* allows students to process what they have read thus far and think deeply about what the author will share in the next segment. For example, as they continue to read about the coming of winter, the students might make the following prediction: "Since the author just spoke about winter coming early, the next segment might be about the rancher making preparations for winter."

The result of such collaboration for the members of these student-led groups is jointly held understandings of the text that the teacher has selected (Palincsar & Brown, 1984). Moreover, the process of creating these jointly held understandings helps to make the text more meaningful for students. Much of the research on RT has involved materials from science or social studies textbooks, and the approach has been successfully used with students in general education and special education.

Scripted Cooperation

Scripted Cooperation (SC) is another well-researched collaborative technique (O'Donnell & Kelly, 1994; Spurlin, Dansereau, Larson, & Brooks, 1984). Like RT, SC is a student-led approach in which the teacher is a participant-observer whose role is to offer support and assistance as needed. Also, the overall goal of SC is to ensure that group members build a shared understanding of the text, problem, or writing assigned to them (O'Donnell & Kelly, 1994).

Despite similarities in purpose and goals for the teacher and the groups, there are several important distinctions between RT and SC. In SC, students work in pairs or dyads, and each member has a role. Specifically, one member of the pair starts out as the recaller, while the other takes the role of listener. The pairs follow a general script that cues these novice facilitators as to the steps they should follow. Students begin by silently reading a prescribed amount of text defined by the teacher, and then the recaller offers a summary of the passage. The role of the listener is to correct or expand this summary.

SC is also unique in that it has an elaboration strategy built into it (Spurlin et al., 1984). After the recaller and listener work together to establish the important content, they are cued to do something additional to improve their memory (e.g., create an explicit or mental picture). Such elaboration promotes students' understandings. It is also hypothesized that the trading of roles between recaller and listener promotes the students' willingness to participate and provides each the opportunity to serve as a source of explanation (O'Donnell & Kelly, 1994).

How Can Instructional Leaders Promote Shared Learning in Classrooms?

Despite the rhetoric about shared learning and teaching, there are many administrators, teachers, and students who remain skeptical about its benefits. In fact, one frequently asked question about socially shared education is whether it translates into better learning for all students. The response to that question depends on the situation and context that surround the learning activity (Gillies, 2003). Overall, the research literature suggests that cooperation or collaboration contribute to increased student achievement and to more positive learning climates (Slavin, 1990). However, these benefits seem to vary based on the abilities of students and their backgrounds (Oakes, 1990; Webb, 1989).

Two important conclusions can be drawn from this literature. The first is that socially shared practices generally promote students' learning and development (Slavin & Oickle, 1981). In addition, the benefits of these practices closely parallel the degree to which groups are adequately planned and facilitated (Sharan, 1994). The take-home message is that putting students in groups to talk is *not* likely to translate into academic gains. We discuss three key factors that will influence the results of socially shared education. Among those factors are: matching the social interaction pattern to the instructional goal; establishing the bases for assessment; and consideration of students' assignment to learning groups.

- ## Social interaction patterns must match instructional goals

The simple fact is that most social learning approaches were created for use under certain conditions or for specific purposes. For instance, Reciprocal Teaching activities center on text processing, while Jigsaw works better with students mature enough to handle independent research. Skillful coordination begins with awareness that all forms of social interaction have potential instructional advantages and disadvantages (Jetton & Alexander, 2000). Those advantages and disadvantages become more evident when we compare fundamental patterns of social interaction (Alexander et al., 1994). As shown in Table 6.3, those six patterns are recitation, open exchange, student-directed learning, student-interactive learning, peer tutoring, and peer learning.

As Alexander and Jetton (2003) have suggested, these six social interaction patterns are basic to any formal or informal approach to socially shared learning. For example, Reciprocal Teaching typically begins with a form of recitation and then moves into student-directed learning. Scripted Cooperation, by comparison, relies on a peer learning pattern. What is important to remember is that none of these social interaction patterns should be considered inherently good or bad (Alexander & Jetton, 2003). Rather, the merits of each depend on whether that pattern is thoughtfully and purposefully instituted and flexibly applied to meet current instructional conditions (Mishler, 1978).

- ## Judgments about socially shared practices should be based on valid and reliable evidence

A problem inherent in using socially shared learning techniques is figuring out whether or not they are working. Unfortunately, it is often difficult to assess whether a particular approach is accomplishing its goals. In essence, teachers need to monitor both the positive and negative effects of these patterns on students' academic, social, and emotional well-being (Fuchs, Fuchs, Hamlet, & Stecker, 1991; Hertz-Lazarowitz & Calderón, 1994). Administrators should help their teachers fine-tune their instructional approaches by collecting and distributing valid and reliable data about socially shared educational practices (Kampwirth, 1999). It also provides educators with important insights as to what types of instructional tasks or activities work well with what types of classroom configuration.

Some of the cooperative learning techniques overviewed in Table 6.2 include very specific mechanisms for student evaluation,

Table 6.3   Comparison of Six Patterns of Classroom Interactions

Type	Description	Cost/Benefit
Recitation	The teacher is the primary source of information, presenting the content and directing questions to students.	Recitation is useful for delivering a large amount of information in a short period of time but limits student engagement.
Open Exchange	Discussion is sparked by a question or dilemma posed by the teacher. The students are then encouraged to converse, with only periodic interjections from the teacher.	An open exchange allows the teacher and students to explore multiple perspectives on an issue but raises the possibility that inaccurate or misleading information will be introduced.
Student-Directed Learning	Students act as surrogate teachers, leading small groups after modeling by the teacher. The teacher assists as needed but has limited involvement.	While student-directed learning leads to students' feelings of increased competence with content, the quality of instruction can be highly variable.
Student-Interactive Learning	Groups of students work together to complete an academic task with no designated leader.	This type of instruction is particularly useful for problem-based activities, but teacher guidance can be highly dispersed.
Peer Tutoring	A student with particular skills and knowledge provides individual instruction to a peer in need of assistance.	Peer tutoring provides individual, one-on-one practice for students with particular needs, but tutees must be willing to receive help from a peer.
Peer Learning	Two partners work together to complete a task or acquire certain knowledge or skills.	This type of interaction is useful for small projects where content is reviewed, but the quality of the learning depends heavily on the pairing of the students.

including worksheets and games that are part of everyday instruction (Johnson & Johnson, 1999; Slavin, 1995). Our suggestion would be to use a wide range of assessment practices that can help you gauge the effect of a social interaction approach. The assessments can be informal or formal and can target areas like student motivation and engagement or knowledge acquisition. For example, a teacher could have students assess the work of their partners, as well as suggest ways to improve the activities.

One caveat in assessing the successfulness or usefulness of a social approach is that it is also important to judge whether students of various abilities, genders, and ethnic groups share equally in that learning (Azmitia, 1988; Slavin & Oickle, 1981). This is particularly important to students who have confronted failure. The social and cultural diversity in many schools lets administrators and teachers consider the effectiveness of instructional practices from multiple vantage points. Specifically, administrators and teachers should be cognizant of any discernible pattern of inequity that arises as a result of a socially shared learning situation. Even though it is unrealistic to assume that all students will benefit equally from each and every instructional activity, persistent inequalities can seriously damage students' continued development (DeVries & Edwards, 1974). Although the collection of academic, motivational, and social data takes time, these forms of data are useful in making instructional decisions about the conditions under which social practices operate optimally.

- **Be sure that the configuration and consistency of the group works for the students**

All of us have found ourselves in groups we would describe as unpleasant or unproductive. We have all come face to face with group members who assume the unhealthy roles of slacker, resister, or dominator (Kagan, 1992). In such cases, it may well be the group's most committed and grade-sensitive student who winds up doing the majority of the work. For these reasons, teachers need to be reflective when forming groups. This is especially the case when those groups will be evaluated as a whole, or when groups will remain together for an extended period of time (Johnson & Johnson, 1994). Key factors to consider when forming groups include ability, personality, gender, or ethnic differences. Some cooperative techniques, such as those developed by Slavin (1995) and Johnson and Johnson (1999), have rather specific procedures for forming mixed-ability and same-ability groups, but other approaches give very little guidance about how groups should be configured. Fuchs and colleagues (1997) have suggested that administrators and teachers vary students by personality, gender, and ethnic differences.

Even when groups are well thought out and seemingly well formed, problems can arise as the school year continues. In such cases, educators might operate under the hope that somehow students will eventually get along. However, groups that are not functioning well need to be assessed quickly so that suitable adjustments can be made. For example, a teacher may avoid putting two students together because they do not seem to get along very well or because both like to be in charge. Having both students in one group would likely be a negative situation for all of the students in their group. Of course, since groups need some time to solidify and settle in, teachers should be careful not to sort or shuffle groups too quickly when minor problems or issues arise (Sharan, 1994).

Change can also be good for groups. Indeed, periodic reassessment of group membership allows for changes in interaction patterns (Hertz-Lazarowitz & Calderón, 1994). The length of group membership should be determined by the tasks to be accomplished and the ongoing health and well-being of the group members. Some flexibility and fluidity in grouping procedures may help maintain student motivation and ward off complacency and stereotyping (Cohen, 1994; Dishon & O'Leary, 1984). As noted, the individual characteristics of the students (e.g., gender or ethnicity) should be taken into consideration when making these important instructional decisions.

Chapter Reflections

If students are going to thrive, administrators and teachers must understand the social and contextual nature of learning. Even though learning will inevitably be social, regardless of the configuration of classrooms, effective administrators and master teachers make social interaction an explicit priority in the school and classroom. In this chapter, we overviewed the nature of shared learning and how the term is often used in the educational literature. In essence, we surmised that the process of learning in schools is necessarily a social process because students acquire knowledge within a social setting in which individuals share ideas.

The second question we addressed concerned the approaches to shared learning that promote achievement. In answering this question, we began by overviewing the characteristics of good discussions—discussions that promote learning and understanding. We also explored an array of cooperative and collaborative procedures that are well researched and that have promising results, including general approaches like Jigsaw and more structured techniques like Reciprocal Teaching. In discussing these approaches, we also contrasted them with approaches that promote competition. Our conclusion was that competition leads to far more negative consequences in classrooms than other collaborative and cooperative techniques.

Finally, we addressed how administrators and teachers can promote socially shared learning in classrooms. In doing so, we offered three guiding principles. Our first guiding principle was that administrators and teachers need to consider their educational goals, the instructional content, as well as the age, ability, and ethnicity of their students when selecting social interaction arrangements. Also, administrators and teachers need to teach students how to be social in a way that promotes the goals of the interaction and affords the opportunity for enhanced academic achievement. Once a particular approach has been implemented, administrators and teachers should secure evaluative information they can trust (i.e., valid and reliable) to judge the effects of the approach on student learning. Such useful data can be found in the course of day-to-day instruction. This essential information comes not only in the form of documented achievements, like scores on a test or assignment, but also in the shape of motivational, social, and behavior data.

Finally, we suggested that it is the role of the administrator to prompt the teacher to continually judge the structure and consistency of student groupings and to assist with behavioral problems that may arise. In doing so, administrators and teachers need to address what factors should be considered in making and maintaining the groups. They also need to determine the point at which the groups should be changed. Administrators and teachers need to routinely answer and review these issues during the course of the year. The bottom line is that socially shared education involves far more than putting desks or students together. It is the result of planful and reasoned educational practice.

7

Concluding
Thoughts

Throughout this volume, we have explored specific questions about development, knowledge, strategies, motivation, and shared learning that should be of tremendous importance to educational leaders concerned with student learning and achievement. Those questions, which initiated each chapter, came directly from teachers and school administrators committed to school improvement and student advancement. Our responses to these questions were framed from decades of psychological research on learning and instruction. Further, each chapter was infused with principles for educational practice that should foster students' academic development, even while promoting their performance on measures of school achievement.

In this era of accountability and high-stakes testing, administrators must be confident that they can foster conditions of learning and instructional expertise so that students can fully develop their capacity and motivation to learn without jeopardizing performance on national and state assessments. Indeed, it has been shown that making student learning, in all its many forms and dimensions, the focus of the educational process will ultimately help produce students who are both able and willing to perform well on achievement measures targeting foundational knowledge and basic skills (Bransford et al., 1999). Thus, administrators need not trade off student learning for higher scores on high-stakes tests. When learning, as broadly addressed in this volume, is the centerpiece of classroom activity, students should not only acquire the basics in reading and mathematics but they should also be able to think deeply and critically in all academic domains.

School administrators play an essential role in creating and maintaining learning communities that serve all constituents—from students to teachers and from parents to community leaders. The goal of this volume has been to look more deeply at student learning and how it unfolds, and to consider the decision making and actions of teachers that serve to advance that learning. Armed with that understanding, school administrators should be better able to identify areas of strength and need, devise instructional interventions, select educational programs and materials, and organize professional development activities that can bring about desired learning outcomes.

Of course, there are no simple solutions or remedies for the present and future challenges that face the educational system. Sometimes it is easy to be drawn into "innovations" or "reforms" (e.g., a focus on learning styles or open schools) that ultimately do not withstand the test of time or hold up against careful scrutiny (Alexander et al., 1996). The cost in time, money, and credibility can be significant in these cases (Cuban et al., 2003). Therefore, educational leaders equipped with knowledge of the psychological research in learning and instruction should be better able to discern evidence-based programs and principles from those built only on promise or conjecture.

The evidence discussed here comes from decades of repeated and systematic studies of learning and pedagogy (Alexander & Murphy, 1998a; APA Board of Educational Affairs, 1995). Sadly, much of that psychological theory and research has remained outside the realm of instructional practice, in part due to psychology's failure to translate theory and research into principles and programs that can operate in the complex and dynamic world of the classroom.

For this volume, we carefully selected topics from the vast psychological literature that have direct implications for educational practice. We then surveyed those topics and forged them into guiding principles that should have broad applicability. Whether the learning environment is primary or secondary, urban or rural, high-achieving or low-performing, the concerns for development, knowledge, motivation, strategies, and shared learning remain constant. Moreover, the principles derived from that research can be adapted to fit the specific needs of districts, schools, and classrooms where the learning truly unfolds.

There is a cautionary tale that must be retold, however. As we sought to make clear in the opening chapter, the dimensions that frame this discussion cannot be treated in isolation. It does little good for administrators to target learning strategies in their schools, for example, instead of helping students gain content knowledge or to make motivation a priority without regard to development and attention to individual differences. These dimensions of learning are truly interrelated. Thus, any effective educational program must incorporate all these dimensions if maximal academic development is the desired outcome. Just as there is no panacea for the challenges faced by students, teachers, and school administrators, there are no shortcuts in this academic journey.

References

Adams, M. J., Treiman, R., & Pressley, M. (1998). Reading, writing, and literacy. In I. Sigel & A. Renninger (Eds.), *Handbook of child psychology: Child psychology in practice* (Vol. 4, pp. 275–355). New York: Wiley.

Afflerbach, P. A., & VanSledright, B. (2001). Hath! Doth! What! The challenges middle school students face when they read innovative history text. *Journal of Adolescent and Adult Literacy, 44,* 696–707.

Alexander, P. A. (1985). Gifted and nongifted students' perceptions of intelligence. *Gifted Child Quarterly, 29,* 137–143.

Alexander, P. A. (1997a). Knowledge-seeking and self-schema: A case for the motivational dimensions of exposition. *Educational Psychologist, 32,* 83–94.

Alexander, P. A. (1997b). Mapping the multidimensional nature of domain learning: The interplay of cognitive, motivational, and strategic forces. In M. L. Maehr & P. R. Pintrich (Eds.), *Advances in motivation and achievement* (Vol. 10, pp. 213–250). Greenwich, CT: JAI Press.

Alexander, P. A. (1998, April). Knowledge seeking: Toward a new model of domain learning. In G. Sinatra (Chair), *New models and metaphors for conceptualizing knowledge.* Invited address at the annual meeting of the American Educational Research Association, San Diego.

Alexander, P. A. (2000). Toward a model of academic development: Schooling and the acquisition of knowledge: The sequel. *Educational Researcher, 29(2),* 28–33, 44.

Alexander, P. A. (2005). *Psychology in learning and teaching.* Columbus, OH: Prentice-Hall.

Alexander, P. A., & Dochy, F. J. R. C. (1995). Conceptions of knowledge and beliefs: A comparison across varying cultural and educational communities. *American Educational Research Journal, 32,* 413–442.

Alexander, P. A., Graham, S., & Harris, K. (1998). A perspective on strategy research: Progress and prospects. *Educational Psychology Review, 10,* 129–154.

Alexander, P. A., & Jetton, T. L. (2000). Learning from text: A multidimensional and developmental perspective. In M. L. Kamil, P. B. Mosenthal, P. D. Pearson, & R. Barr (Eds.), *Handbook of reading research* (Vol. III, pp. 285–310). Mahwah, NJ: Lawrence Erlbaum Associates.

Alexander, P. A., & Jetton, T. L. (2003). Learning from traditional and alternative texts: New conceptualization for an information age. In A. Graesser, M. Gernsbacher, & S. Goldman (Eds.), *Handbook of discourse processes* (pp. 199–241). Mahwah, NJ: Lawrence Erlbaum Associates.

Alexander, P. A., Jetton, T. L., Kulikowich, J. M., & Woehler, C. (1994). Contrasting instructional and structural importance: The seductive effects of teacher questions. *Journal of Reading Behavior, 26,* 19–45.

Alexander, P. A., & Judy, J. E. (1988). The interaction of domain-specific and strategic knowledge in academic performance. *Review of Educational Research, 58,* 375–404.

Alexander, P. A., & Murphy, P. K. (1993). The research base for APA's learner-centered psychological principles. In N. M. Lambert & B. L. McCombs (Eds.), *Issues in school reform: A sampler of psychological perspectives on learner-centered schools* (pp. 33–60). Washington, DC: American Psychological Association.

Alexander, P. A., & Murphy, P. K. (1998a). Profiling the differences in students' knowledge, interest, and strategic processing. *Journal of Educational Psychology, 90,* 435–447.

Alexander, P. A., & Murphy, P. K. (1998b). The research base for APA's learner-centered principles. In N. M. Lambert & B. L. McCombs (Eds.), *Issues in school reform: A sampler of psychological perspectives on learner-centered school* (pp. 25–60). Washington, DC: The American Psychological Association.

Alexander, P. A., Murphy, P. K., & Kulikowich, J. M. (1998). What responses to domain-specific analogy problems reveal about emerging competence: A new perspective on an old acquaintance. *Journal of Educational Psychology, 90,* 397–406.

Alexander, P. A., Murphy, P. K., & Woods, B. S. (1996). Of squalls and fathoms: Navigating the seas of educational innovation. *Educational Researcher, 25(3),* 31–36, 39.

Alexander, P. A., Schallert, D. L., & Hare, V. C. (1991). Coming to terms: How researchers in learning and literacy talk about knowledge. *Review of Educational Research, 61,* 315–343.

Alexander, P. A., Willson, V. L., White, C. S., Fuqua, J. D., Clark, G. D., Wilson, A. F., et al. (1989). Development of analogical reasoning in four- and five-year-old children. *Cognitive Development, 4,* 65–88.

Allen, M., Hale, J., Mongeau, P., Berkowits-Stafford, S., Stafford, S., Shanahan, W., Agee, P., Dillon, K., Jackson, R., & Ray, C. (1994). Testing a model of message sidedness: Three replications. *Communication Monographs, 57,* 274–291.

Allington, R. (1980). Teacher interruption behaviors during primary-grade oral reading. *Journal of Educational Psychology, 71,* 371–377.

Alvermann, D. E., Smith, L. C., & Readence, J. E. (1985). Prior knowledge activation and the comprehension of compatible and incompatible text. *Reading Research Quarterly, 20,* 420–436.

American Psychological Association Board of Educational Affairs. (1995, December). *Learner-centered psychological principles: A framework for school redesign and reform.* [Online]. Available at: www.apa.org/ed/lcp.html.

Ames, C. (1984). Competitive, cooperative, and individualistic goal structures: A motivational analysis. In R. Ames & C. Ames (Eds.), *Research on motivation in education* (Vol. 1, pp. 177–207). New York: Academic Press.

Ames, C. (1992). Classrooms: Goals, structures, and student motivation. *Journal of Educational Psychology, 84,* 261–271.

Ames, C., & Ames, R. (Eds.). (1989). *Research on motivation in education: The classroom milieu* (Vol. 3). San Diego: Academic Press.

Ames, C., & Archer, J. (1988). Achievement goals in the classroom: Students' learning strategies and motivation processes. *Journal of Educational Psychology, 80(3),* 260–267.

Anderson, J. R. (1983). *The architecture of cognition.* Cambridge, MA: Harvard University.

Anderson, R. C., Chinn, C., Chang, J., Waggoner, J., & Yi, H. (1997). On the logical integrity of children's arguments. *Cognition and Instruction, 15(2),* 135–167.

Anderson, R. C., Reynolds, R. E., Schallert, D. L., & Goetz, E. T. (1977). Frameworks for comprehending discourse. *American Educational Research Journal, 14,* 367–381.

Anderson, T. H., & Armbruster, B. B. (1984). Studying. In P. D. Pearson, R. Barr, M. L. Kamil, & P. Mosenthal (Eds.), *Handbook of reading research,* (Vol. I, pp. 657–679). White Plains, NY: Longman.

Anderson, T. H., & Armbruster, B. B. (1986). *The value of taking notes* (Reading Education Report No. 374). Champaign, IL: University of Illinois at Urbana-Champaign, Center for the Study of Reading.

Armbruster, B. B. (2000). Taking notes from lectures. In R. F. Flippo & D. C. Caverly (Eds.), *Handbook of college reading and study strategy research* (pp. 175–199). Mahwah, NJ: Lawrence Erlbaum Associates.

Aronson, E. (1978). *The jigsaw classroom.* Beverly Hills, CA: Sage.

Aronson, E., Blaney, N., Sikes, J., Stephan, C., & Snapp, M. (1978). *The jigsaw classroom.* Beverly Hills, CA: Sage.

Aronson, E., & Patnoe, S. (1997). *The jigsaw classroom* (2nd ed.). New York: Longman.

Astington, J. W. (1993). *The child's discovery of the mind.* Cambridge, MA: Harvard University Press.

Azmitia, M. (1988). Peer interaction and problem solving: When are two heads better than one? *Child Development, 59,* 87–96.

Badderly, A. D. (1982). *Your memory: A user's guide.* New York: Macmillan.

Bandura, A. (1977). Self-efficacy: Toward a unifying theory of behavioral change. *Psychological Review, 84,* 191–215.

Bandura, A. (1982). Self-efficacy mechanism in human agency. *American Psychologist, 37,* 122–147.

Bandura, A. (1986). *Social foundations of thought and action.* Englewood Cliffs, NJ: Prentice-Hall.

Bandura, A., & Schunk, D. H. (1981). Cultivating competence, self-efficacy, and intrinsic interest through proximal self-motivation. *Journal of Personality and Social Psychology, 41,* 586–598.

Bangert-Drowns, R. L., Kulik, C. C., Kulik, J. A., & Morgan, M. (1991). The instructional effects of feedback in test-like events. *Review of Educational Research, 61,* 213–238.

Bazerman, C. (1981). What written knowledge does: Three examples of academic discourse. *Philosophy of the Social Sciences, 11,* 361–387.

Bergin, D. A., Ford, M. E., & Hess, R. D. (1993). Patterns of motivation and social behavior associated with microcomputer use of young children. *Journal of Educational Psychology, 85,* 437–445.

Berk, L. E. (1999). *Infants and children: Prenatal through middle childhood* (3rd ed.). Boston: Allyn & Bacon.

Blumenfeld, P. C. (1992). Classroom learning and motivation: Clarifying and expanding goal theory. *Journal of Educational Psychology, 84(3),* 272–281.

Bong, M. (1996). Problems in academic motivation research and advantages and disadvantages of their solutions. *Contemporary Educational Psychology, 21,* 149–165.

Borkowski, J. G., Carr, M., & Pressley, M. (1987). "Spontaneous" strategy use: Perspectives from metacognitive theory. *Intelligence, 11,* 61–75.

Bransford, J. D., Brown, A. L., & Cocking, R. R. (1999). *How people learn: Brain, mind, experience, and school.* Washington, DC: National Academy Press.

Bredekamp, S. (1987). *Developmentally appropriate practices in early childhood programs serving children from birth through age 8.* Washington, DC: National Association for the Education of Young Children.

Bronfenbrenner, U. (1979). *The ecology of human development.* Cambridge, MA: Harvard University Press.

Brophy, J. (1998). *Motivating students to learn.* Boston: McGraw-Hill.

Brophy, J. (1999). Toward a model of the value aspects of motivation in education: Developing appreciation for particular learning domains and activities. *Educational Psychologist, 34,* 75–85.

Brophy, J., & Good, T. (1986). Teacher behavior and student achievement. In M. Wittrock (Ed.), *Handbook of research on teaching* (3rd ed., pp. 328–375). New York: Macmillan.

Brophy, J., & VanSledright, B. (1997). *Teaching and learning history in elementary schools.* New York: Teachers' College Press.

Brown, A. L. (1975). The development of memory: Knowing, knowing about knowing, and knowing how to know. In H. W. Reese (Ed.), *Advances in child development and behavior* (Vol. 10, pp. 103–152). New York: Academic Press.

Brown, A. L., & Campione, J. S. (1990). Communities of learning and thinking, or a context by any other name. *Contributions to Human Development, 21,* 108–126.

Brown, A. L., & Palinscar, A. S. (1987). Reciprocal teaching of comprehension strategies: A natural history of one program for enhancing learning. In J. Borkowski & J. D. Day (Eds.), *Cognition in special education: Comparative approaches to retardation, learning disabilities, and giftedness.* Norwood, NJ: Ablex.

Brown, A. L., & Palincsar, A. S. (1989). Guided, cooperative learning and individual knowledge acquisition. In L. B. Resnick (Ed.), *Knowing, learning, and instruction: Essays in honor of Robert Glaser* (pp. 393–451). Hillsdale, NJ: Erlbaum.

Brown, J. S., Collins, A., & Duguid, P. (1989). Situated cognition and the culture of learning. *Educational Researcher, 18(1),* 32–42.

Brown, M. R., Paulsen, K., & Higgins, K. (2003). 20 ways to remove environmental barriers to student learning. *Intervention in School and Clinic, 39,* 109–112.

Butler, R. (1994). Teacher communications and student interpretations: Effects of teacher responses to failing students on attributional inferences in two age groups. *British Journal of Educational Psychology, 64,* 277–294.

Byrnes, J. P. (1996). *Cognitive development and learning in instructional contexts.* Boston: Allyn & Bacon.

Byrnes, J. P. (2001). *Cognitive development and learning in instructional contexts* (2nd ed.). Boston: Allyn & Bacon.

Campione, J. C., Shapiro, A. M., & Brown, A. L. (1995). Forms of transfer in a community of learners: Flexible learning and understanding. In A. McKeough, J. Lupart, & A. Marini (Eds.), *Teaching for transfer: Fostering generalization in learning* (pp. 35–68). Mahwah, NJ: Lawrence Erlbaum.

Carey, S. (1985). *Conceptual change in childhood.* Cambridge, MA: MIT Press.

Carnegie Council on Adolescent Development. (1996). *Great transitions: Preparing adolescents for a new century (Abridged Version).* New York: Carnegie Corporation.

Case, R. (1993). Theories of learning and theories of development. *Educational Psychologist, 28,* 219–233.

Caverly, D. C., Orlando, V. P., & Mullen, J. L. (2000). Textbook study reading. In R. F. Flippo & D. C. Caverly (Eds.), *Handbook of college reading and study strategy research* (pp. 105–147). Mahwah, NJ: Lawrence Erlbaum Associates.

Cazden, C. (1988). *Classroom discourse: The language of teaching and learning.* Portsmouth, NJ: Heinemann.

Chambliss, M. J. (1995). Text cues and strategies successful readers use to construct the gist of lengthy written arguments. *Reading Research Quarterly, 30,* 778–807.

Chambliss, M. J., & Garner, R. (1996). Do adults change their minds after reading persuasive text? *Written Communication, 13,* 291–313.

Chambliss, M. J., & Murphy, P. K. (2002). Fourth and fifth graders representing the argument structure in written texts. *Discourse Processes, 34,* 91–115.

Chinn, C. A., & Brewer, W. F. (1993). The role of anomalous data in knowledge acquisition: A theoretical framework and implications for science instruction. *Review of Educational Research, 63,* 1–49.

Chiu, S., & Alexander, P. A. (2000). The motivational function of preschoolers' private speech. *Discourse Processes, 30,* 133–152.

Cognition and Technology Group at Vanderbilt. (1996). Looking at technology in context: A framework for understanding technology and education research. In D. C. Berliner & R. C. Calfee (Eds.), *Handbook of educational psychology* (807–840). New York: Macmillan.

Cohen, E. G. (1994). Restructuring the classroom: Conditions for productive small groups. *Review of Educational Research, 64,* 1–36.

Cole, M., Gay, J., Glick, J. A., & Sharp, D. W. (1971). *The cultural context of learning and thinking.* New York: Basic Books.

Cowan, N. (1995). *Attention and memory.* New York: Oxford University Press.

Creed, P. A., Muller, J., & Patton, W. (2003). Leaving high school: The influences and consequences for psychological well-being and career-related confidence. *Journal of Adolescence, 26,* 295–311.

Csikszentmihalyi, M. (1990). *FLOW: The psychology of optimal experience.* New York: HarperCollins.

Cuban, L., Usdan, M. D., & Hale, E. L. (2003). *Powerful reforms with shallow roots: Improving America's urban schools.* New York: Teacher's College Press.

Cuffaro, H. (1991). A view of materials as the texts of the early childhood curriculum. In B. Spodek & O. Saracho (Eds.), *Issues in early childhood curriculum* (pp. 64–85). New York: Teachers College Press.

Damon, W. (1983). *Social and personality development: Infancy through adolescence.* New York: W. W. Norton.

Damon, W., & Hart, D. (1988). *Self-understanding in childhood and adolescence.* New York: Cambridge University Press.

de Jong, T., & van Joolingen, W. R. (1998). Scientific discovery learning with computer simulations of conceptual domains. *Review of Educational Research, 68,* 179–201.

Deutsch, M. (1949). The effects of cooperation and competition upon group processes. *Human Relations, 2,* 199–231.

Deutsch, M. (1993). Educating for a peaceful world. *American Psychologist, 48,* 510–517.

Deutsch, W., & Pechmann, T. (1982). Social interaction and the development of definite descriptions. *Cognition, 11,* 159–184.

DeVries, D., & Edwards, K. (1974). Student teams and learning games: Their effects on cross-race and cross-sex interaction. *Journal of Educational Psychology, 66,* 741–749.

Dewey, J. (1913). *Interest and effort in education.* Boston: Riverdale.

Dewey, J. (1930). Conduct and experience. In C. Murchism (Ed.), *Psychologies of 1930* (pp. 410–429). Worcester, MA: Clark University Press.

Dienes, Z., & Berry, D. (1997). Implicit learning: Below the subjective threshold. *Psychonomic Bulletin & Review, 4,* 3–23.

Dishon, D., & O'Leary, P. (1984). *Guidebook for cooperative learning.* Holmes Beach, FL: Learning Publications.

Doyle, W. (1983). Academic work. *Review of Educational Research, 53,* 159–200.

Duit, R., & Treagust, D. F. (2003). Conceptual change: A powerful framework for improving science teaching and learning. *International Journal of Science Education, 25,* 671–688.

Dweck, C. (1986). Motivational processes affecting learning. *American Psychologist, 41,* 1040–1048.

Dweck, C., & Leggett, E. (1988). A social-cognitive approach to motivation and personality. *Psychological Review, 95(2),* 256–273.

Eccles, J. S., & Midgley, C. (1990). Changes in academic motivation and self-perceptions during early adolescence. In R. Montemayor, G. R. Adams, & T. P. Gullotta (Eds.), *Advances in adolescent development: From childhood to adolescence* (Vol. 2, pp. 134–155). Newbury Park, CA: Sage.

Eccles, J. S., Midgley, C., & Adler, T. (1984). Grade-related changes in the school environment: Effects on achievement motivation. In J. Nicholls (Ed.), *Advances in motivation and achievement* (Vol. 3, pp. 283–331). Greenwich, CT: Jai Press.

Eccles, J. S., Wigfield, A., & Schiefele, U. (1998). Motivation to succeed. In W. Damon (Series Ed.) & N. Eisenberg (Vol. Ed.), *Handbook of Child Psychology* (Vol. 3, pp. 1017–1095). New York: Wiley.

Elawar, M. C., & Corno, L. (1985). A factorial experiment in teachers' written feedback on student homework: Changing teacher behavior a little rather than a lot. *Journal of Educational Psychology, 77,* 162–173.

Ellis, H. C., & Hunt, R. R. (1983). *Fundamentals of human memory and cognition,* 3rd ed. Dubuque, IA: W. C. Brown.

English, L. D. (1997). *Mathematical reasoning: Analogies, metaphors, and images.* Mahwah, NJ: Lawrence Erlbaum Associates.

Entwisle, D. R., & Baker, D. P. (1983). Gender and young children's expectations for performance in arithmetic. *Developmental Psychology, 19,* 200–209.

Ericsson, K. A., & Simon, H. A. (1980). Verbal reports as data. *Psychological Review, 87,* 215–251.

Erikson, E. H. (1963). *Childhood and society* (2nd ed.). New York: Norton.

Erikson, E. H. (1980). *Identity, youth, and crisis* (2nd ed.). New York: W. W. Norton.

Fives, H., & Alexander, P. A. (2001). Teaching as persuasion: A case in point. *Theory into Practice, 40,* 242–248.

Flavell, J. H. (1987). Speculation about the nature and development of metacognition. In F. E. Weinert & R. H. Kluwe (Eds.), *Metacognition, motivation, and understanding* (pp. 21–29). Hillsdale, NJ: Erlbaum.

Flavell, J. H., Miller, P. H., & Miller, S. A. (1993). *Cognitive development* (3rd ed.). Englewood Cliffs, NJ: Prentice-Hall.

Ford, M. E. (1992). *Motivating humans: Goals, emotions, and personal agency.* Newbury Park, CA: Sage.

Freebody, P., & Anderson, R. C. (1983). Effects of vocabulary difficulty, text cohesion, and schema availability on reading comprehension. *Reading Research Quarterly, 18(3),* 277–294.

Fuchs, D., Fuchs, L. S., Hamlett, C. L, & Stecker, P. M. (1991). Effects of curriculum-based measurement and consultation on teacher planning and student achievement in mathematics operations. *American Educational Research Journal, 28,* 617–641.

Fuchs, D., Fuchs, L. S., Mathes, P. G., & Simmons, D. C. (1997). Peer-assisted learning strategies: Making classrooms more responsive to diversity. *American Educational Research Journal, 34,* 174–206.

Fuchs, L. S., Fuchs, D., Prentice, K., Burch, M., Hamlet, C. L., Owen, R., et al. (2003). Enhancing third-grade students' mathematical problem solving with self-regulated learning strategies. *Journal of Educational Psychology, 95,* 306–315.

Garner, R. (1987). *Metacognition and reading comprehension.* Norwood, NJ: Ablex.

Garner, R. (1990). When children and adults do not use learning strategies: Toward a theory of setting. *Review of Educational Research, 60,* 517–529.

Gaskill, P., & Murphy, P. K. (2004). Effects of a memory strategy on second-graders' self-efficacy. *Contemporary Educational Psychology, 29,* 27–49.

Geary, D. C. (1994). *Children's mathematical development.* Washington, DC: American Psychological Association.

Gillies, R. M. (2003). The behaviors, interactions, and perceptions of junior-high school students during small-group learning. *Journal of Educational Psychology, 95,* 137–147.

Gilligan, C. (1977). In a different voice: Women's conceptions of self and morality. *Harvard Educational Review, 47,* 481–517.

Ginott, H. (1972). *Teacher and child.* New York: Macmillan.

Ginzberg, E. (1972). Toward a theory of occupational choice: A restatement. *Vocational Guidance Quarterly, 20,* 169–176.

Glaser, R. (1984). Education and thinking: The role of knowledge. *American Psychologist, 39,* 93–104.

Goals 2000: Educate America Act. (1994, March 31). Pub. Law 103–227 (108 Stat. 125).

Goetz, E. T., Alexander, P. A., & Ash, M. (1992). *Educational psychology: A classroom perspective.* Columbus, OH: Charles E. Merrill.

Goswami, U. (1992). *Analogical reasoning in children.* Hillsdale, NJ: Lawrence Erlbaum Associates.

Graham, S. (1984). Communicating sympathy and anger to Black and White children: The cognitive (attributional) consequences of affective cues. *The Journal of Personality and Social Psychology, 47,* 14–28.

Graham, S., & Weiner, B. (1996). Theories and principles of motivation. In D. C. Berliner & R. C. Calfee (Eds.), *Handbook of educational psychology* (pp. 63–84). New York: Macmillan.

Graves, M. F. (1997, March). *What sort of comprehension strategy instruction should schools provide?* Symposium presented at the annual meeting of the American Educational Research Association, Chicago.

Grotevant, H. D., Cooper, C. R., & Kramer, K. (1986). Exploration as a predictor of congruence in adolescents' career choices. *Journal of Vocational Behavior, 29,* 201–215.

Guzzetti, B., & Hynd, C. (1998). *Theoretical perspectives on conceptual change.* Mahwah, NJ: Lawrence Erlbaum Associates.

Hardre, P. L., & Reeve, J. (2003). A motivational model of rural students' intentions to persist in, versus drop out of, high school. *Journal of Educational Psychology, 95,* 347–356.

Hare, V. C., & Borchardt, K. M. (1984). Direct instruction of summarization skills. *Reading Research Quarterly, 20(1),* 62–78.

Harris, K. R., & Alexander, P. A. (Eds.) (1998). Integration, constructivist education [Special Issue]. *Educational Psychology Review, 10(2).*

Harris, K. R., & Graham, S. (1996). *Making the writing process work: Strategies for composition and self-regulation.* Cambridge, MA: Brookline.

Harter, S. (1996). Teacher and classmate influences on scholastic motivation, self-esteem, and level of voice in adolescents. In J. Juvonen & K. Wentzel (Eds.), *Social motivation: Understanding children's school adjustment* (pp. 11–42). New York: Cambridge University Press.

Hastie, R., & Pennington, N. (1991). Cognitive and social processes in decision making. In L. B. Resnick, J. M. Levine, & S. D. Teasley (Eds.), *Perspectives on socially shared cognition* (pp. 308–327). Washington, DC: American Psychological Association.

Heath, S. (1983). *Ways with words: Language, life, and work in communities and classrooms.* New York: Cambridge University.

Heath, S. B. (1991). "It's about winning!" The language of knowledge in baseball. In L. B. Resnick, J. M. Levine, & S. D. Teasley (Eds.), *Perspectives on socially shared cognition* (pp. 101–124). Washington, DC: American Psychological Association.

Hertz-Lazarowitz, R., & Calderón, M. (1994). Facilitating teachers' power through collaboration: Implementing cooperative learning in elementary schools. In S. Sharan (Ed.), *Handbook of cooperative learning methods* (pp. 300–317). Westport, CT: Praeger.

Hidi, S. (1990). Interest and its contribution as a mental resource for learning. *Review of Educational Research, 60,* 549–571.

Hidi, S., & Anderson, V. (1992). Situational interest and its impact on reading and expository writing. In K. A. Renninger, S. Hidi, & A. Krapp (Eds.), *The role of interest in learning and development* (pp. 215–238). Hillsdale, NJ: Erlbaum.

Hynd, C. (2001). Persuasion and its role in meeting educational goals. *Theory into Practice, 40,* 270–277.

Hynd, C., Alvermann, D., & Qian, G. (1997). Preservice elementary school teachers' conceptual change about projectile motion: Refutation text, demonstration, affective factors, and relevance. *Science Education, 81,* 1–27.

Inhelder, B., & Piaget, J. (1958). *The growth of logical thinking from childhood to adolescence.* New York: Basic Books.

James, W. (1890). *Principles of psychology* (Vols. 1 & 2). New York: Holt.

Jetton, T. L. (1994). *Teachers' and students' understanding of scientific exposition: How importance and interest influence what is accessed and what is discussed.* Unpublished doctoral dissertation. College Station, TX: Texas A & M University.

Jetton, T.L., & Alexander, P.A. (2000, January). *The nature of student involvement: Discussion genres that occur in science classrooms.* Manuscript submitted for publication.

Johnson, D. W., & Johnson, R. T. (1994). *Learning together and alone* (2nd ed.). Englewood, NJ: Prentice-Hall.

Johnson, D. W., & Johnson, R. T. (1999). *Learning together and alone: Cooperative, competitive, and individualistic learning.* Boston: Allyn & Bacon.

Johnson, D. W., Johnson, R. T., & Stanne, M. B. (2000). *Cooperative learning methods: A meta-analysis.* [Online]. Available at www.clcrc.com/pages/cl-methods.html

Juel, C. (1988). Learning to read and write: A longitudinal study of 54 children from first through fourth grades. *Journal of Educational Psychology, 80,* 417–447.

Kagan, S. (1992). *Cooperative learning.* San Juan Capistrano, CA: Resources for Teachers.

Kagan, S., & Kagan, M. (1994). The structural approach: Six keys to cooperative learning. In S. Sharan (Ed.), *Handbook of cooperative learning methods* (pp. 115–133). Westport, CT: Praeger.

Kampwirth, T. J. (1999). *Collaborative consultation in the schools.* Upper Saddle River, NJ: Merrill.

Kantor, R., Green, J., Bradley, M., & Lin, L. (1992). The construction of schooled discourse repertoires: An interactional sociolinguistic perspective on learning to talk in preschool. *Linguistics in Education, 4,* 131–172.

Kapinus, B., & Haynes, J. A. (1983). *Effects of prior knowledge, text-order, and underlining on recall of information from text.* (ERIC Document Reproduction Service No. ED 237 968).

Karabenick, S. A. (2004). Perceived achievement goal structure and college student help seeking. *Journal of Educational Psychology, 96,* 569–581.

Kierwa, K. A. (1989). A review of note taking: The encoding-storage paradigm and beyond. *Educational Psychology Review, 1,* 147–172.

Kohlberg, L. (1975). The cognitive-developmental approach to moral education. *Phi Delta Kappan, 56,* 670–677.

Kohlberg, L. (1976). Moral stages and moralization: The cognitive-developmental approach to socialization. In J. Lickona (Ed.), *Moral development behavior: Theory, research and social issues.* New York: Holt, Rinehart and Winston.

Kohlberg, L. (1981). *The philosophy of moral development: Moral stages and the idea of justice.* San Francisco: Harper & Row.

Kohn, A. (1993). *Punished by rewards: The trouble with gold stars, incentive plans, A's, praise, and other bribes.* Boston: Houghton Mifflin.

Kostelnik, M. (1992). Myths associated with developmentally appropriate practice. *Young Children, 47*(4), 17–25.

Kuhn, T. (1970). *The structure of scientific revolutions* (2nd ed). Chicago: Chicago University Press.

Lemke, J. L. (1990). *Talking science: Language, learning and values.* Norwood, NJ: Ablex.

Levin, J. R. (1993). Mnemonic strategies and classroom learning: A twenty-year report card. *Elementary School Journal, 94,* 235–244.

Lipman, M. (1991). *Thinking in education.* New York: Cambridge University Press.

Lipson, M. (1983). The influence of religious affiliation on children's memory for text information. *Reading Research Quarterly, 18,* 448–457.

Lipson, M. (1995). The effect of semantic mapping instruction on prose comprehension of below-level college readers. *Reading Research and Instruction, 34,* 367–378.

Locke, J. (1938). *Some thoughts concerning education.* London: Churchill. (Original published in 1699.)

Loentiev, A. N. (1981). *Problems in the development of mind.* Moscow: Progress.

Luft, J. (1970). *Group processes: An introduction to group dynamics* (2nd ed.). Palo Alto, CA: National Press Books.

Maehr, M. (1982). *Motivational factors in school achievement.* Paper commissioned by the National Commission on Excellence in Education. (NIE 400-81-0004, Task 10).

Maehr, M. L., & Anderman, E. M. (1993). Reinventing schools for early adolescents: Emphasizing task goals. *Elementary School Journal, 93,* 593–610.

Maier, S. F., & Seligman, M. E. P. (1976). Learned helplessness: Theory and evidence. *Journal of Experimental Psychology, 105,* 3–46.

Maslow, A. H. (1954). *Motivation and personality.* New York: Harper & Row.

Mason, L. (1996). An analysis of children's construction of new knowledge through their use of reasoning and arguing in classroom discussions. *International Journal of Qualitative Studies in Education, 9*(3), 411–433.

Maxim, G. W. (2003). Let the fun begin! Dynamic social studies for the elementary classroom. *Childhood Education, 80,* 2–5.

McCaslin, M., & Good, T. L. (1996). The informal curriculum. In D. C. Berliner & R. C. Calfee (Eds.), *Handbook of educational psychology* (pp. 622–670). New York: Macmillan.

Meece, J. L., Blumenfeld, P. C., & Hoyle, R. (1988). Students' goal orientations and cognitive engagement in classroom activities. *Journal of Educational Psychology, 80,* 514–523.

Meece, J. L., & Holt, K. (1993). A pattern analysis of students' achievement goals. *Journal of Educational Psychology, 85*(4), 582–590.

Mehan, H. (1979). *Learning lessons: Social organization in the classroom.* Cambridge MA: Harvard University Press.

Miller, G. A. (1956). The magical number seven, plus or minus two: Some limits on our capacity for processing information. *Psychological Review, 63,* 81–97.

Miller, R. B., Behrens, J. T., Greene, B. A., & Newman, D. (1993). Goals and perceived ability: Impact on students valuing, self-regulation, and persistence. *Contemporary Educational Psychology, 18,* 2–14.

Miller, R. B., Greene, B. A., Montalvo, G. P., Ravindran, B., & Nichols, J. D. (1996). Engagement in academic work: The role of learning goals, future consequences, pleasing others, and perceived ability. *Contemporary Educational Psychology, 21,* 388–422.

Miserandino, M. (1996). Children who do well in school: Individual differences in perceived competence and autonomy in above-average children. *Journal of Educational Psychology, 88,* 203–214.

Mishler, E.G. (1978). Studies in dialogue and discourse: III. Utterance structure and utterance function in interrogative sequences. *Journal of Psycholinguistic Research, 7,* 279–305.

Montessori, M. (1964). *The Montessori method.* New York: Schocken Books.

Morrow, L. M. (1997). *Literacy development in the early years: Helping children to read and write* (3rd ed.). Boston: Allyn & Bacon.

Munuchin, P. P., & Shapiro, E. K. (1983). The school as a context of social development. In P. H. Mussen (Ed.), *Handbook of child psychology* (Vol. 4, 4th ed.). New York: Wiley.

Murphy, P. K. (1998). *Toward a multifaceted model of persuasion: Exploring textual and learner interactions.* Unpublished doctoral dissertation. College Park, MD: College of Education, University of Maryland.

Murphy, P. K. (2001, April). *Strategic processing of informational texts in the information age.* Symposium presented at the annual meeting of the American Educational Research Association, Seattle, Washington.

Murphy, P. K., & Alexander, P. A. (2000). A motivated look at motivational terminology. *Contemporary Educational Psychology, 25,* 3–53.

Murphy, P. K., & Alexander, P. A. (2002). The learner-centered principles: Their value for teachers and teaching. In W. D. Hawley (Ed.), *KEYS to school improvement* (pp. 10–27). Washington, DC: National Education Association.

Murphy, P. K., & Alexander, P. A. (2004). Persuasion as a dynamic, multidimensional process: An investigation of individual and intraindividual differences. *American Educational Research Journal, 41,* 337–363.

Murphy, P. K., Long, J. F., Holleran, T. A., & Esterly, E. (2003). Persuasion online or on paper: A new take on an old issue. *Learning and Instruction, 13*(5), 511–532.

Murphy, P. K., & Mason, L. (in press). Changing knowledge and changing beliefs. In P. A. Alexander & P. Winne (Eds.), *Handbook of Educational Psychology* (2nd ed.). New York: Lawrence Erlbaum.

Murphy, P. K., Wilkinson, I., & Soter, A. (2004, April). *Making sense of group discussions: A conceptual framework.* Paper presented at the annual meeting of the American Educational Research Association, San Diego.

Nafpaktitis, M., Mayer, G., & Butterworth, T. (1985). Natural rates of teacher approval and disapproval and their relation to student behavior in intermediate school classrooms. *Journal of educational psychology, 77(3)*, 362–367.

National Commission of Excellence in Education. (1983). *A nation at risk: The imperative for educational reform.* Washington, DC: U.S. Government Printing Office.

Natriello, G., & Dornbusch, S. (1985). *Teacher evaluative standards and student effort.* New York: Longman.

Newman, R. S., & Goldin, L. (1990). Children's reluctance to seek help with school-work. *Journal of educational psychology, 82(1)*, 92–100.

Nicholls, J. G. (1989). *The competitive ethos and democratic education.* Cambridge, MA: Harvard University Press.

Nicholls, J. G., & Miller, R. B. (1994). Cooperative learning and student motivation. *Contemporary Educational Psychology, 19*, 167–178.

Nicholls, J. G., Patashnick, M., & Nolen, S. B. (1985). Adolescents' theories of education. *Journal of Educational Psychology, 77*, 683–692.

Nichols, J. D. (1996). The effects of cooperative learning on student achievement and motivation in a high school geometry class. *Contemporary Educational Psychology, 21*, 467–476.

Nystrand, M. (2003). *Opening dialogue: Understanding the dynamics of language and learning in the English classroom.* New York: Teachers College Press.

Oakes, J. (1990). *Multiplying inequalities: The effects of race, social class, and tracking on opportunities to learn mathematics and science* (Report No. R-3928-NSF). Santa Monica, CA: Rand Corp.

O'Donnell, A. M., & Kelly, J. (1994). Learning from peers: Beyond the rhetoric of positive results. Educational Psychology Review, 6, 321–350.

Ogbu, J. (1974). *The next generation: An ethnography of education in an urban neighborhood.* New York: Academic Press.

Pajares, M. F. (1992). Teachers' beliefs and educational research: Cleaning up a messy construct. *Review of Educational Research, 62*, 307–332.

Palincsar, A. S., & Brown, A. L. (1984). Reciprocal teaching of comprehension-fostering and monitoring activities. *Cognition and Instruction, 1*, 117–175.

Paris, S. G., & Cunningham, A. E. (1996). Children becoming students. In D. C. Berliner & R. C. Calfee (Eds.), *Handbook of educational psychology* (pp. 117–147). New York: Macmillan.

Paris, S. G., Lipson, M. Y., & Wixson, K. K. (1983). Becoming a strategic reader. *Contemporary Educational Psychology, 8*, 293–316.

Paris, S. G., Wasik, B. A., & Turner, J. C. (1991). The development of strategic readers. In R. Barr, M. L. Kamil, P. Mosenthal, & P. D. Pearson (Eds.), *Handbook of reading research* (Vol. II, pp. 609–640). Mahwah, NJ: Lawrence Erlbaum Associates.

Pellegrini, A. D. (1988). Elementary-school children's rough-and-tumble play and social competence. *Developmental Psychology, 24*, 802–806.

Perkins, D. N. (1992). *Smart schools: Better thinking and learning for every child.* New York: The Free Press.

Perkins, D. N., & Simmons, R. (1988). Patterns of misunderstanding: An integrative model for science, math, and programming. *Review of Educational Research, 58*, 303–326.

Pesa, J. (1999). Psychsocial factors associated with dieting behaviors among female adolescents. *Journal of School Health, 69*(5), 196–200.

Peterson, C., Maier, S., & Seligman, M. (1993). *Learned helplessness: A theory for the age of personal control.* New York: Oxford University Press.

Petty, R. E., & Cacioppo, J. T. (1986). *Communication and persuasion: Central and peripheral routes to attitude change.* New York: Springer-Verlag.

Phillips, G. M. (1973). *Communication and the small group* (2nd ed.). New York: Bobbs-Merrill Company.

Piaget, J. (1930). *The child's conception of physical causality.* New York: Harcourt, Brace.

Piaget, J. (1952). *The origins of intelligence in children.* (M. Cook trans.). New York: W. W. Norton.

Piaget, J. (1955). *The language and thought of the child.* (M. Gabain, trans.). New York: Noonday Press.

Piaget, J., Montanegro, J., & Billeter, J. (1977). Les correlats. In J. Piaget (Ed.), *L'Abstraction Reflechissante.* Paris: Presses Universitaires de France.

Pintrich, P. R. (2003). A motivational science perspective on the role of student motivation in learning and teaching constructs. *Journal of Educational Psychology, 95,* 667–686.

Pintrich, P. R., & Schunk, D. H. (1996). *Motivation in education: Theory, research, and applications.* Englewood Cliffs, NJ: Merrill-Prentice Hall.

Pintrich, P. R., & Schunk, D. H. (2001). *Motivation in education: Theory, research, and applications* (2nd ed.). Englewood Cliffs, NJ: Prentice Hall.

Prawat, R. S. (1989). Promoting access to knowledge, strategy, and disposition in students: A research synthesis. *Review of Educational Research, 59,* 1–41.

Pressley, M., & Afflerbach, P. A. (1995). *Verbal protocols of reading: The nature of constructively responsive reading.* Hillsdale, NJ: Lawrence Erlbaum Associates.

Pressley, M., Goodchild, F., Fleet, J., Zajchowski, R., & Evans, E. D. (1989). The challenges of classroom strategy instruction. *Elementary School Journal, 89,* 301–342.

Pressley, M., Levin, J. R., & Delaney, H. D. (1982). The mnemonic keyword method. *Review of Educational Research, 52,* 61–92.

Pressley, M., & McCormick, C. B. (1995). *Cognition, teaching, and assessment.* New York: HarperCollins.

Pugach, M. C., & Johnson, L. J. (1995). *Collaborative practitioners, collaborative schools.* Denver: Love.

Rabinowitz, M., & Chi, M. T. H. (1987). An interactive mode of strategic processing. In S. J. Ceci (Ed.), *Handbook of cognitive, social, and neuropsychological aspects of learning disabilities.* Hillsdale, NJ: Erlbaum.

Radziszewska, B., & Rogoff, B. (1988). Influence of adult and peer collaborators on children's planning skills. *Developmental Psychology, 24,* 840–848.

Reeve, J. (1996). *Motivating others: Nurturing inner motivational resources.* Boston: Allyn and Bacon.

Reimann, P., & Schult, T. J. (1996). Turning examples into cases: Acquiring knowledge structures for analogical problem solving. *Educational Psychologist, 31*(2), 123–132.

Reynolds, R. E., & Shirey, L. L. (1988). The role of attention in studying and learning. In C. E. Weinstein, E. T. Goetz, & P. A. Alexander (Eds.), *Learning and study strategies: Issues in assessment, instruction, and evaluation* (pp. 77–100). San Diego, CA: Academic Press.

Roberton, M. A. (1984). Changing motor patterns during childhood. In J. R. Thomas (Ed.), *Motor development during childhood and adolescence* (pp. 48–90). Minneapolis, MN: Burgess.

Rock, D. A., Owings, J. A., & Lee, R. (1994). *Changes in math proficiency between eighth and tenth grades.* Washington, DC: National Center for Education Statistics.

Rogoff, B. (1990). *Apprenticeship in thinking: Cognitive development in social context.* New York: Oxford University Press.

Romance, N. R., & Vitale, M. R. (1992). A curriculum strategy that expands time for in-depth elementary science instruction by using science-based reading strategies: Effects of a year-long study in grade four. *Journal of Research in Science Teaching, 29,* 545–554.

Rosenblatt, L. M. (1978). *The reader, the text, the poem.* Carbondale, IL: Southern Illinois University.

Rousseau, J. J. (1911). *Emile: Or on education.* London: Dent. (Original published in 1762).

Rubin, K. H., Fein, G. G., & Vandenberg, B. (1983). Play. In E. M. Hetherington (Ed.), *Handbook of child psychology: Vol. 4, Socialization, personality, and social development* (4th ed., pp. 693–744). New York: Wiley.

Rumelhart, D. E. (1980). Schemata: The building blocks of cognition. In R. J. Spiro, B. C. Bruce, & W. F. Brewer (Eds.), *Theoretical issues in reading comprehension* (pp. 33–58). Hillsdale, NJ: Lawrence Erlbaum Associates.

Rumelhart, D. E., & Norman, D. A. (1981). Accretion, tuning, and restructuring: Three modes of learning. In J. W. Cotton & R. Klatzy (Eds.), Semantic factors in cognition (pp. 37–60). Hillsdale, NJ: Lawrence Erlbaum Associates.

Ryan, R. M., & Deci, E. L. (2000). Intrinsic and extrinsic motivations: Classic definitions and new directions. *Contemporary Educational Psychology, 25,* 54–67.

Ryle, G. (1949). *The concept of mind.* London: Hutchinson.

Sadker, M., & Sadker, D. (1994). *Failing at fairness: How America's schools cheat girls.* New York: Scribner.

Sadker, M., Sadker, D., & Klein, S. (1991). The issue of gender in elementary and secondary education. *Review of Research in Education, 17,* 269–334.

Salomon, G. (1991). Transcending the qualitative-quantitative debate: The analytic and systemic approach to educational research. *Educational Psychologist, 20*(6), 10–18.

Scarr, S. (1992). Developmental theories for the 1990s: Development and individual differences. *Child Development, 63,* 1–19.

Schiefele, U. (1991). Interest, learning, and motivation. *Educational Psychologist, 26,* 229–323.

Schön, D. A. (1988). Designing: Rules, types, and words. *Design Studies, 9,* 181–190.

Schunk, D. H. (2000). Coming to terms with motivation constructs. *Contemporary Educational Psychology, 25,* 116–119.

Scrimsher, S., & Tudge, J. (2003). The teaching/learning relationship in the first few years of school: Some revolutionary implications of Vygotsky's theory. *Early Education and Development, 14,* 293–312.

Seifert, K. L., Hoffnung, R. J., & Hoffnung, M. (1997). *Lifespan development.* Boston: Houghton Mifflin.

Seligman, M. E. P. (1975). *Helplessness: On depression, development, and death.* San Francisco: Freeman.

Sharan, S. (1994). Cooperative learning and the teacher. In S. Sharan (Ed.), Handbook of cooperative learning methods (pp. 136–348). Westport, CT: Praeger.

Sharan, Y., & Sharan, S. (1992). *Expanding cooperative learning through group investigation.* New York: Teachers' College Press.

Shuell, T. J. (1986). Cognitive conceptions of learning. *Review of Educational Research, 56,* 411–436.

Shweder, R. A., Mahapatra, M., & Miller, J. G. (1990). Culture and moral development. In J. W. Stigler, R. A. Shweder, & G. Herdt (Eds.), *Cultural psychology: Essays on comparative human development.* Cambridge, England: Cambridge University Press.

Sigelman, C. K., & Shaffer, D. R. (1995). *Life-span human development* (2nd ed.). Pacific Grove, CA: Brooks/Cole Publishing.

Slavin, R. E. (1990). Ability grouping and student achievement in secondary schools: A best-evidence synthesis. *Review of Educational Research, 60,* 471–499.

Slavin, R. E. (1995). *Cooperative learning: Theory, research, and practice* (2nd ed.). Boston: Allyn and Bacon.

Slavin, R. E., Leavey, M. B., & Madden, N. A. (1985). *Team Assisted Individualization: Mathematics.* Watertown, MA: Charlesbridge.

Slavin, R. E., & Oickle, E. (1981). Effects of cooperative learning teams on student achievement and race relations: Treatment by race interactions. *Sociology of Education, 54,* 174–180.

Spencer, V. G., Scruggs, T. E., & Mastropieri, M. A. (2003). Content area learning in middle school social studies classrooms and students with emotional or behavioral disorders: A comparison of strategies. *Behavioral Disorders, 28,* 77–93.

Spielberger, C. D. (1998). Foreword. In N. M. Lambert & B. L. McCombs (Eds.), *How students learn: Reforming schools through learner-centered education* (pp. ix–xi). Washington, DC: American Psychological Association.

Spiro, R. J., Feltovich, P. J., Jacobson, M. J., & Coulson, R. L. (1992). Cognitive flexibility, constructivism, and hypertext: Random access instruction for advanced knowledge acquisition in ill-structured domains. In T. M. Duffy & D. H. Jonassen (Eds.), *Constructivism and the technology of instruction: A conversation* (pp. 57–75). Cambridge, UK: Cambridge University Press.

Spurlin, J. E., Dansereau, D. F., Larson, C. O., & Brooks, L. W. (1984). Cooperative learning strategies in processing descriptive text: Effects of role and activity level of the learner. *Cognition and Instruction, 1,* 451–463.

Stanovich, K. E. (1986). Matthew effects in reading: Some consequences of individual differences in the acquisition of literacy. *Reading Research Quarterly, 21,* 360–407.

Sternberg, R. J. (1977). *Intelligence, information processing, and analogical reasoning: The componential analysis of human abilities.* Hillsdale, NJ: Lawrence Erlbaum Associates.

Sternberg, R. J. (1985). *Beyond IQ: A triarchic theory of human intelligence.* New York: Cambridge University Press.

Sternberg, R. J., & Wagner R. K. (1986). *Practical intelligence.* Cambridge, UK: Cambridge University Press.

Stipek, D. J. (1988). *Motivation to learn: From theory to practice.* Englewood Cliffs, NJ: Prentice Hall.

Stipek, D. J. (1993). *Motivation to learn: From theory to practice* (2nd ed.). Boston: Allyn & Bacon.

Stipek, D. J. (1996). Motivation and instruction. In D. C. Berliner & R. C. Calfee (Eds.), *Handbook of educational psychology* (pp. 85–113). New York: Macmillan.

Stipek, D. J., & Gralinski, J. H. (1996). Children's beliefs about intelligence and school performance. *Journal of Educational Psychology, 88(3),* 397–407.

Tanner, J. M. (1990). *Fetus into man: Physical growth from conception to maturity* (2nd ed.). Cambridge, MA: Harvard University Press.

Tanner, J. M. (1991). Adolescent growth spurt. In R. M. Lerner, A. C. Peterson, & J. Brooks-Gunn (Eds.), *Encyclopedia of adolescence* (Vol. 1, pp. 419–424). New York: Garland.

Tekkaya, C. (2003). Remediating high school students' misconceptions concerning diffusion and osmosis through concept mapping and conceptual change text. *Research in Science and Technical Education, 21,* 5–16.

Toulmin, S. E. (1958). *The uses of argument.* Cambridge, UK: Cambridge University Press.

U. S. Department of Health and Human Services (1994). *Creating a 21st century Head Start: Final report of the advisory committee on Head Start quality and expansion.* Washington, DC: U. S. Government Printing Office.

VanSledright, B. (1996). Closing the gap between school and disciplinary history? *Advances in Research on Teaching* (Vol. 6, pp. 257–289). Greenwich, CT: JAI Press.

Vosniadou, S. E. (1994). Capturing and modeling the process of conceptual change. *Learning and Instruction, 4,* 45–69.

Voss, J. F., Blais, J., Means, M. L., Greene, T. R., & Ahwesh, E. (1986). Informal reasoning and subject matter knowledge in the solving of economics problems of naive and novice individuals. *Cognition and Instruction, 3,* 269–302.

Vygotsky, L. S. (1978). *Mind in society.* Cambridge, MA: Harvard University Press.

Vygotsky, L. S. (1986). *Thought and language.* (A. Kozulin, Trans.). Cambridge, MA: MIT Press. (Original work published in 1934.)

Wade, S. E. (1992). How interest affects learning from text. In K. A. Renninger, S. Hidi, & A. Krapp (Eds.), *The role of interest in learning and development* (pp. 255–277). Hillsdale, NJ: Lawrence Erlbaum Associates.

Walker, S. N., Sechrist, K. R., & Pender, N. J. (1987). The health-promoting lifestyle profile: Development and psychometric characteristics. *Nursing Journal, 36,* 76–81.

Webb, N. M. (1989). Peer interaction and learning in small groups. *International Journal of Educational Research, 13,* 21–40.

Webb, N. M., & Palincsar, A. S. (1996). Group processes in the classroom. In D. C. Berliner & R. C. Calfee (Eds.), *Handbook of educational psychology* (pp. 841–873). New York: Macmillan.

Weiner, B. (1972). *Theories of motivation: From mechanism to cognition.* Chicago: Markham.

Weiner, B. (1986). *An attributional theory of motivation and emotion.* New York: Springer-Verlag.

Weiner, B. (1991). On perceiving the other person as responsible. In R. A. Dienstbier (Ed.), *Nebraska symposium on motivation* (Vol. 38, pp. 165–198). Lincoln, NE: University of Nebraska Press.

Weiner, B. (1994). Ability versus effort revisited: The moral determinants of achievement evaluation and achievement as a moral system. *Educational Psychologist, 29,* 163–172.

Weiner, B., Graham, S., & Chandler, C. (1982). Pity, anger, and guilt: An attributional analysis. *Personality and Social Psychology Bulletin, 8,* 226–232.

Weinstein, C. E., & Mayer, R. E. (1986). The teaching of learning strategies. In M. C. Wittrock (Ed.), *Handbook of research on teaching* (3rd ed., pp. 315–327). New York: Macmillan.

Wellman, H. M., & Gelman, S. A. (1998). Knowledge acquisition in foundational domains. In D. Kuhn & R. S. Siegler (Eds.), *Handbook of child psychology* (5th ed.), Vol. 2, *Cognition, perception, and language* (pp. 523–573). New York: Wiley.

Wentzel, K. R. (1989). Adolescent classroom goals, standards for performance, and academic achievement: An interactionist perspective. *Journal of Educational Psychology, 81,* 131–142.

Wentzel, K. R. (1991). Social and academic goals at school: Achievement motivation in context. In M. L. Maehr & P. R. Pintrich (Eds.), *Advances in motivation and achievement* (Vol. 7, pp. 185–212). Greenwich, CT: JAI Press, Inc.

Wentzel, K. R. (1996). Social and academic motivation in middle school: Concurrent and longterm relations in academic effort. *Journal of Early Adolescence, 16,* 390–406.

Wentzel, K. R. (1999). Social-motivational processes and interpersonal relationships: Implications for understanding motivation at school. *Journal of Educational Psychology, 91,* 76–97.

Wentzel, K. R. (2000). What is it that I'm trying to achieve? Classroom goals from a content perspective. *Contemporary Educational Psychology, 25,* 105–115.

Wertsch, J. V. (1985). *Vygotsky and the social formation of mind.* Cambridge MA: Harvard University Press.

White, C. S., & Coleman, M. (2000). *Early childhood education: Building a philosophy for teachers.* Columbus, OH: Merrill/Prentice Hall.

Whitehurst, G. J., & Lonigan, C. (1998). Child development and emergent literacy. *Child Development, 69,* 848–872.

Wigfield, A. (1993). Why should I learn this? Adolescents' achievement values for different activities. In In M. L. Maehr & P. R. Pintrich (Eds.), *Advances in motivation and achievement* (Vol. 8, pp. 99–138). Greenwich, CT: JAI Press, Inc.

Wigfield, A., & Eccles, J. S. (1992). The development of achievement task values: A theoretical analysis. *Developmental Review, 12,* 265–310.

Wigfield, A., & Eccles, J. S. (2000). Expectancy-value theory of achievement motivation. *Contemporary Educational Psychology, 25,* 68–81.

Wigfield, A., Eccles, J. S., & Pintrich, P. R. (1996). Development between the ages of 11 and 25. In D. Berliner & R. Calfee (Eds.), *Handbook of educational psychology* (pp. 148–185). New York: Macmillan.

Winne, P. H. (1995). Inherent details in self-regulated learning. *Educational Psychologist, 30,* 173–187.

Wlodkowski, R. (1985). *Enhancing adult motivation to learn.* San Francisco: Jossey-Bass.

Woolfolk, A.E. (2001). *Educational psychology* (8th ed.). Boston: Allyn & Bacon.

Youniss, J., & Smollar, J. (1989). Adolescents' interpersonal relationships in social context. In T. J. Berndt & G. Ladd (Eds.), *Peer relationships in child development* (pp. 300–316). New York: Wiley.

Zimmerman, B. J. (1990). Self-regulated learning and academic achievement: An overview. *Educational Psychologist, 21,* 3–18.

Zimmerman, B. J. (1995). Self-regulation involves more than metacognition: A social cognitive perspective. *Educational Psychologist, 30,* 217–221.

Zimmerman, B. J., & Martinez-Pons, M. (1992). Perceptions of efficacy and strategy use in the self-regulation of learning. In D. H. Schunk & J. L. Meece (Eds.), *Student perceptions in the classroom* (pp. 185–207). Hillsdale, NJ: Lawrence Erlbaum Associates.

Zuckerman, D. (1999). Research watch: Girls just aren't having fun. *Youth Today, 8(4),* 10–12.

Index

NOTE: Page numbers in *italics* indicate tables and figures.

**CORWIN
PRESS**

The Corwin Press logo—a raven striding across an open book—represents the union of courage and learning. Corwin Press is committed to improving education for all learners by publishing books and other professional development resources for those serving the field of PreK–12 education. By providing practical, hands-on materials, Corwin Press continues to carry out the promise of its motto: **"Helping Educators Do Their Work Better."**

A co-publication with the American Association of School Administrators, the Leadership for Learning series is centered on student learning and is aligned with the Interstate School Leaders Licensure Consortium (ISLLC) and National Policy Board for Educational Administration (NPBEA) standards. Authored by leading experts, the series addresses the knowledge and capabilities that have been identified as essential for effective leadership in schools. Each volume in the series blends research, theory, and lessons from practice to help principals and other educational leaders solve the most critical challenges facing their schools. At a time when educators must implement research-based solutions to critical problems, this series is an important step towards keeping improved student achievement at the center of any accountability effort.